GETTING
JUSTICE
WRONG

NICHOLAS COWDERY

GETTING JUSTICE WRONG

MYTHS, MEDIA AND CRIME

ALLEN & UNWIN

Allen & Unwin
83 Alexander St
Crows Nest NSW 2065
Australia
Phone: (61 2) 8425 0100
Fax: (61 2) 9906 2218
Email: frontdesk@allen-unwin.com.au
Web: http://www.allenandunwin.com

National Library of Australia
Cataloguing-in-Publication entry:

Cowdery, Nicholas.
    Getting justice wrong : myths, the media and crime.

    Includes index.
    ISBN 1 86508 322 4.

    1. Mass media and criminal justice — Australia. 2. Crime
and the press — Australia. I. Title.

343.94099

Set in 10.5/14 Garamond by Midland Typesetters Pty Ltd
Printed by Australian Print Group, Maryborough Vic.

10 9 8 7 6 5 4 3 2 1

Contents

I want public servants to provide information that ministers need to hear. I want them to always be conscious of the public good, so that when they are confronted with the choice they can argue for the public good as vigorously as their circumstances allow, rather than following a political line.

TONY HARRIS
Former NSW Auditor General

Law and order is an easy thing for politicians to push . . .

JEFF SHAW QC
Former NSW Attorney General

Preface

*If I were to try to read, much less answer,
all the attacks made on me, this shop might
as well be closed for any other business. I do
the very best I know how — the very best I
can; and I mean to keep doing so until the
end. If the end brings me out all right, what
is said against me won't amount to
anything. If the end brings me out wrong,
ten thousand angels swearing I was right
would make no difference.*

ABRAHAM LINCOLN

In a former life (not in the Shirley MacLaine sense) I practised as a barrister — doing, amongst other things, criminal defence work. I would like a dollar for every time I was asked by a non-lawyer: 'But how can you defend him, knowing that he's guilty?'

When I moved into my present role the non-lawyer questions changed. They are now often asked by journalists and talkback radio commentators, the 'opinionated entertainers', and of course by politicians. The questions are different but they still arise from ignorance of the criminal justice system, how it operates and what it is properly capable of achieving in a democratic society under the rule of law. Ignorance and myths are perpetuated — and with them the false expectations of the public. Of course, this suits the purposes of those now asking the questions (and often supplying their own answers).

In his 1841 book *Extraordinary Popular Delusions and the Madness of Crowds* Charles Mackay wrote: 'Men think in herds; it will be seen that they go mad in herds, while they only recover their senses slowly, and one by one.' Talkback radio knows this. Politicians know this. They seek to make us mad at election times and leave us to recover between them. We are presently between elections.

As Foster Meharny Russell said, 'Every story has three sides to it — yours, mine and the facts'. This book arose out of an invitation by the publishers to consider examining fairly briefly and succinctly a few of the perennial and some of the more fashionable myths about aspects of the criminal justice process, much as I had done in occasional speeches and articles. It has wandered off that track somewhat, but the myths that are confronted in this book are of the kind usually trotted out by politicians at election times and fuelled by sections of the media, most notably the tabloid press, low IQ television, and talkback radio. As Oscar Wilde once observed: 'By giving us the opinions of the uneducated, modern journalism keeps us in touch with the ignorance of the community.' I was happy to accept the invitation, although, with a day job, it has taken a while to fulfil it.

In 1965 Spike Milligan wrote *A Book of Bits or a Bit of a Book* — this could be similarly described (but without Spike's wit). Even this inadequate effort, I hope, may help our community in the long term to recognise misinformation and dumb reaction, to acknowledge facts and to accept and support policies based upon reality and guided by common sense (which is not as common as it should be).

* * *

Today's tabloid newspapers are tomorrow's garbage wrappers or recycled pulp. Low IQ television is usually immediately recognisable for what it is. There is a greater danger in talkback radio — politicians feed off it (even now, after the Australian Broadcasting Authority's inquiry into Sydney Radio 2UE and its 'entertainers' John Laws and Alan Jones) — and politicians make public policy.

In 1990 the former Australian Broadcasting Tribunal said with masterly understatement: 'Talkback encourages robust debate on issues by people who are not fully informed.' Most politicians do not try to fill that information gap before they, too, join in that robust debate. But even those who do try, are caught up in the broadcasters' game. Talkback hosts do not consider the public interest and how public policy may serve it (as politicians should). They are concerned only with making money — for themselves and then for their employers. They do so by fuelling what Hugh Mackay describes as the age of anxiety. John Laws, a so-called 'king' of talkback radio, has said: 'I'm not a journalist and I don't pretend to be a journalist. I'm an entertainer ... there isn't a hook for ethics.' You said it, John!

This book is not an analysis based upon rigorous scientific research. It is not an official government report or a political polemic. It is certainly not a complete treatment of the topics it addresses. Each chapter, and sometimes a part of a chapter, could probably become a book in itself, and some related (and important) topics are not covered at all. Rather, it tries to present some facts, information and especially food for thought. Maybe, just maybe, it can help to put paid to the 'law and order auctions' that seem to have become a feature of state election campaigns.

While any royalties from this publication will go to the

Office of the Director of Public Prosecutions for New South Wales (henceforth 'DPP' — it needs the money!), all views expressed are purely personal. They do not necessarily reflect the official or unofficial views of the Office, any other government agency or any person other than the author. In the nature of the subject, not everything stated can be original and a lot of it has been said or written before by me or by someone else.

But it is obviously necessary to say it again!

One: The Criminal Law in Action

> *Let reverence for the laws be breathed by*
> *every ... mother to the lisping babe that*
> *prattles on her lap; let it be taught in*
> *schools, seminaries, and in colleges; let it be*
> *written in primers, spelling books and in*
> *almanacs; let it be preached from the pulpit,*
> *proclaimed in legislative halls, and enforced*
> *in courts of justice. And, in short, let it*
> *become the political religion of the nation.*
>
> ABRAHAM LINCOLN (again)

> *Well, I say good riddance to bad rubbish.*
> *That's three less car thieves. I think they're*
> *dead and I think that's good.*
>
> HOWARD SATTLER

Horrific crimes make for horrific reporting. There are some horrifying reporters about. Exceptional cases allow the commentators to say exceptional things and some people watching grabs on television, listening to talkback opinion-mongers or reading the short words and phrases of tabloid crusaders might gain the perception that all crime in the courts is like that. It is not. People hear nothing about most of the crime that occurs because it does not make sensational news.

Crime is everywhere and nobody is immune from it. Since humankind first ordered its society by setting rules there have been rule-breakers and there always will be. While a crime-free society is a worthy goal, history and common experience teach us that it is unattainable. The best we can hope to achieve is an acceptable level of crime control, balancing police measures against the freedom to be enjoyed in an open society. And while crime continues, all of us are at some risk of being affected by it. That is an unavoidable fact and we must all learn to live with it — and, if we can, to minimise our risk.

Sometimes that prospect produces fear or apprehension. Nobody chooses or likes to be a victim of crime. Those who seek the approval and support of the community — (opposition) politicians especially — play upon that fear. It is in their interests first to *exaggerate* the problem and then to propose solutions or cures for it, as if they alone have the power to alter reality. Because they are addressing people who, for the most part, have no detailed knowledge of the issues involved, they talk in simple black-and-white terms. That brings easy public recognition and engagement. The problems are painted black and the solutions white. But in reality there are few black-and-white propositions in this area. The problems, the issues and the solutions come in all shades of grey, the politicians' least favoured colour (but one that government politicians resort to readily whenever they are asked to provide proof that their 'solutions' are actually working).

Talkback commentators also love black-and-white pictures.

Those with knowledge of the criminal justice process and of its place in society protest against this simplified picture. They also have an interest in informing the public, but as fully and accurately as possible. That is difficult to do in the era of the sound bite and shortened attention spans. Their arguments are not simple, and not black and white, because they know that is not the nature of the problem, the issues or the solutions. They do their best in a measured, considered and detailed way, but such attempts get little exposure. Ignorance boosts the ratings and the circulation figures. Those who know find it difficult to compete against those who apparently do not.

So what is there to know? How is it, for example, that our present system has come about?

Over centuries society has put rules in place and established ways of dealing with the rule-breakers. Those methods have been modified by experience, by trial and error. As the responsibility for law enforcement passed to the state — the sovereign or executive government — an imbalance of power was created. The state, with all its resources, prosecuting in its own courts, brings its full weight against (usually) an individual of limited power and means. Without procedural safeguards — checks in place at all stages of proceedings against an individual — there is the potential for injustice to occur.

As our numbers have grown and the structure of our community and its institutions and its activities have become more complex, the systems and processes — and the safeguards — have also had to become more complex and detailed. They have also had to respond to standards set internationally by bodies such as the United Nations (see Chapter 9 The Island Continent).

The first and most important safeguard of the rights of you, the individual, against any misuse of the power of the state, is the existence of the third arm of government — an independent judiciary.

The three separate arms of government are the *legislature* (the Parliament which makes the laws), the *executive* (the ministers and the government departments under their administration) and the *judiciary* (the courts, comprising judges and magistrates). In our system of government the three arms are intended to be independent of each other, not subject to inappropriate influence by another. For example, the executive (including ministers and bureaucrats) cannot tell the courts (the judges) how to decide cases. Nor can the Parliament.

This separation is demonstrated within the courtroom. In criminal cases the executive power is the prosecutor. The prosecutor cannot also be the judge: you cannot have somebody making allegations and also deciding if those allegations are true. There are rules to ensure that the judiciary exists and acts independently of the executive. It also acts independently of the legislature (Parliament), the lawfulness of whose conduct it sometimes has to judge in cases brought before the courts. Another example of this separation of powers in practice is that the courts, not the Parliament (the legislature), must impose penalties for criminal offending — although they do so within ranges set by the legislature (see Chapter 8 Sentencing).

Another safeguard for the individual is the presumption of innocence. An accused person is presumed to be innocent unless and until proven guilty in court. We have an adversarial system in this country where the state is one party in contest against another party, the individual accused person. They are adversaries. The dice would be loaded unfairly if the accused was presumed to be guilty and had to prove innocence.

In practical terms, the presumption of innocence means that the party bringing the allegation must prove it (the 'onus of proof'). In criminal cases the standard of proof that must be reached is proof beyond reasonable doubt. That is an expression that judges, by law, may not explain any more fully to juries. People are assumed to know what it means. (In civil cases — court hearings of non-criminal matters, such as claims for compensation or commercial disputes — the standard of proof is the balance of probabilities. Oddly, juries in those cases can be told what that means.)

Operational and procedural safeguards for the individual apply to the police (and other investigative agencies, which are part of the executive) and the courts. It might be said that there is a series of *gateways* through which a suspected or accused person must pass on the journey to conviction and punishment. Unless each gateway is negotiated satisfactorily, the journey stops and the suspect or accused goes free. The reason for the existence of the gateways is the prevention of injustice and abuse of the weak at the hands of the strong (the community at large). The gateways are there to attempt to ensure fairness in the criminal justice process — but it must be fairness to both the accused and the community. A balance is always required when fairness is to be achieved and sometimes it is difficult to strike the right one. If that balance isn't struck — or seen to be struck — that is when we hear howls like John Laws' 'Australia's judicial system is really a joke today . . .' or the Chief Minister and Attorney General of the Northern Territory's extraordinary declaration in 2000 that the justice system is 'totally corrupt'.

The system can always be improved, but the process of reform is inherently cautious. It moves more slowly than some people might want, but that may be no bad thing. People's rights are being affected in significant ways and we should not be anxious to rush into mistakes. We should resist demands for instant change for the sake of change — an alteration in one respect is likely to have effects elsewhere, not all of which may be foreseeable at the time. We should be careful not to create a monster worse than we already have.

We have now a criminal justice process that begins with complaint and ends with punishment. Rules determine what tests must be applied (and by whom) and how the gateways are to be negotiated at each stage through the system. So let's go through the sequence of gateways and see how they operate.

COMPLAINT

The criminal justice process typically begins with a complaint by a victim of crime or an observer, usually to the police. The complaint (or action by a police officer) begins the investigation. There are some circumstances (for example, in some cases of sexual assault) in which the speed with which a complaint is made after the event may enable the complaint itself to be evidence in proof of the crime in court.

INVESTIGATION

Police investigate crime. (There are some other investigative agencies for particular types of crime.) They record the complaint, take statements from persons with relevant knowledge, examine places or premises where the offence is alleged to have occurred, and search for evidence (such as fingerprints, physical evidence or signs left behind, documents, records and so on). If a suspect is identified (perhaps having been apprehended at the scene, identified by the victim or found in possession of stolen property, for example) then he or she is interviewed, or at least given the option of being interviewed.

Once upon a time suspects were tortured until they confessed (or died). These days we acknowledge the inherent dignity of the human person and the existence of human rights that preserve that dignity, including the right of every person not to be subjected to torture. In any event, confessions extracted by torture are highly likely to be unreliable — that is, untrue — things said just to end the torture. For similar reasons, confessions that result from threats, inducements or improper pressure of any kind are rejected and cannot be acted on by the courts. To be accepted into evidence a confession must be the result of the suspect's exercise of a free choice to speak or to remain silent. Rules have been made for determining whether or not that is likely to have been the case, and there are special rules for those the law determines are not adults or of full capacity, or are likely to be especially vulnerable (such as children, Aborigines or intellectually disabled people). Because they are vulnerable they are more susceptible to pressure by persons in authority.

There are strict limits on the powers of police to detain a suspect in custody during an investigation. Police cannot arrest a person simply for questioning. Broadly speaking, a person may only be arrested (detained against his or her will) if caught committing certain offences or if police already have reasonable cause to suspect the person of having committed or being about to commit certain offences.

A suspect may decline to be interviewed, may say a little or may say a lot. Some or all of what is said may be admitted into evidence in court, subject to the rules of evidence that apply. Whether charged or not, a suspect is entitled to seek legal advice and representation at every stage of the proceedings.

Once a suspect is charged and becomes a 'defendant' (someone who may defend a charge made in court) in the Magistrates Court a decision has to be made about whether or not he or she will be locked up or let free. The defendant may be held in custody awaiting a prompt court appearance or may be granted bail — conditional liberty — either by police at the time of charge or by a court at the first appearance or upon later application.

It is important to understand that the tests applied to determine whether or not a person is let free before any conviction are quite different from the tests that apply to freedom after conviction. In the former case the main question is whether or not the defendant will *appear* at court on the next occasion he or she is required to do so. There may also be a need to consider whether the public needs to be protected from the person or whether a witness may be in danger if the person is released. After conviction, however, the court must consider the appropriate *punishment* to be imposed. The giving or withholding of bail has nothing to do with punishment. When bail is being considered before conviction the person is still presumed to be innocent and is not liable to criminal punishment. After conviction, bail may be granted before sentence, especially if the sentence (or punishment) is not likely to be a gaol sentence.

PROSECUTION

Once police compile a brief of evidence (including statements from witnesses and the exhibits to be tendered) a prosecutor must decide whether or not it is sufficient to support the prosecution of the charge — whether or not there is a *reasonable prospect of conviction* that would justify proceeding further with the case. If a police officer or the prosecutor decides that there should be a charge, the prosecution commences at that point. The test to be applied at this first stage — or gateway — by a police officer is whether or not the evidence supports a reasonable suspicion that the person committed the offence.

In cases of serious (indictable) crime the Office of the DPP conducts the prosecution. If it is a less serious (summary) charge, police prosecutors still do so in New South Wales in most cases. (This is changing across the country and the DPP will take over this role.) In the Office of the DPP the brief is constantly reviewed, or screened, with continual assessments being made of the prospects of conviction. This judgment — as are all other prosecution decisions made in the Office — is made in accordance with the DPP's *Prosecution Policy and Guidelines* (a document that is freely and publicly available). Police prosecutors sometimes claim that they apply the *Policy and Guidelines*, but in my observation often they do not. DPP prosecutors have far more discretion to pursue the justice of a case than do police prosecutors under the more rigid police procedures. Police tend to go for the highest possible penalties rather than a punishment that is sufficient; and police prosecutors cannot negotiate as DPP lawyers can. (That is merely one more reason why it is inappropriate to have police still filling the role of prosecutors in the Local Court.)

If a DPP prosecutor decides (following the appropriate internal Office procedures) that there is no reasonable prospect of conviction by a reasonable jury (or judge or magistrate) properly instructed as to the law, then the prosecution is discontinued. Detailed reasons for such action are usually not provided, although a brief indication of the reason may be given in cases of public interest or where it is requested by an interested (i.e. involved) party. Any decision to discontinue a prosecution is always open to later review if further evidence emerges or if circumstances otherwise change in a material way. The decision does not necessarily mean that there will never be a prosecution — it is not a finding that the offence was not committed and it does not have the status of an acquittal after a trial.

COMMITTAL PROCEEDINGS

Unless the DPP discontinues it, the prosecution proceeds. The bulk of criminal cases are for minor offences and they are dealt with in the Local Court. There defendants may plead guilty or may opt for a defended hearing.

In a case of serious (indictable) crime which is triable in a higher court (in New South Wales the District or Supreme Court), a magistrate of the Local Court conducts an administrative hearing called a committal proceeding. The purpose is to inquire into the evidence available and to determine whether or not, on that evidence, it can be said that there is a reasonable prospect that a jury would convict — another test applied at this gateway in the proceedings. The magistrate does not make any finding about guilt and the extent to which the evidence can be tested or rejected is limited. Again there are rules governing these procedures, designed to preserve the essential rights of the defendant but also in part to give some measure of protection to any victims. The magistrate's reasons for the finding are usually contained in a short judgment.

Like all judicial officers, magistrates are not in a position to make comments outside the court about particular cases they hear. Court sittings are open to the public (with few very strict exceptions, and then mainly where children are involved) and judicial officers are required to explain their reasons for decisions in the course of the hearings. It is a completely open and accountable process, able to be observed and reported upon by anybody. The justification for action taken by all judicial officers is to be found in the records of the proceedings themselves. There is certainty, transparency and public confidence in the outcome, which could be weakened by unstructured and selective comment after the event.

A magistrate's finding in a committal proceeding is not binding on the DPP (whose Office has the conduct of the matter from committal proceeding to trial and any appeal). A magistrate may commit for trial but the DPP may decide, in accordance with the *Prosecution Policy and Guidelines*, that there is *no* reasonable prospect of conviction (the converse of the test applied by the magistrate — who looks for a reasonable prospect of conviction — also constituting another gateway) and discontinue the matter. Conversely, a magistrate may discharge a defendant but the DPP may decide that an *ex officio* indictment (one laid although there has been no committal for trial) should nevertheless be laid in the higher court and a trial proceed. Disagreement between the magistrate and the DPP does not necessarily mean that one is 'right' and the other 'wrong' — it is simply the making of a different judgment upon the basis of the existing evidence at the time the decision is made. Committal proceedings are, nevertheless, an effective screening or filtering process and as such constitute a useful gateway along the criminal path. They require an objective judicial assessment to be made of the case brought by the authorities before a defendant is subjected to the risk and cost of a trial. Within the strict limits prescribed, the evidence produced by the prosecution is tested before the magistrate. The defendant may or may not give and/or call evidence at that stage. If the defendant does give evidence or calls a witness, they may be cross-examined by the prosecutor. In the vast majority of cases only the prosecution evidence is presented and mostly it is done with documents.

TRIAL

At any stage of the court process the person charged may plead guilty and be dealt with on an agreed set of facts (or facts proved beyond reasonable doubt, if some of them are not agreed). That may happen in the Local Court or later in a higher court. In some circumstances the Local Court may proceed to impose a penalty; in other circumstances it may commit the person for sentence to the District or Supreme Court. Sometimes a charge bargain may occur — that is, a plea of guilty to a lesser or different charge from the one first brought may be accepted and the person dealt with on that charge (in the Local Court, if possible, but otherwise in the higher court). There are strict requirements for such a bargain and the charge which does proceed must reflect the overall criminality involved in the offending and give to the sentencing court adequate scope for the imposition of an appropriate penalty. It is not unknown for police to 'charge high' in order to encourage the negotiation of a plea of guilty to a lesser charge.

If the defendant maintains a plea of not guilty and is committed for trial, the 'defendant' in the Local Court becomes (simply by convention) the 'accused' in the trial court. The District Court tries all cases but murder and a few others that go to the Supreme Court. At no stage is the accused required to make a contribution to the proceedings (see Chapter 7 What Right to Silence?). If he or she stays silent throughout, a plea of not guilty will be entered and the same requirements of proof as in any other case will be imposed upon the prosecution. No adverse inference (a conclusion against the interests of the accused) may be drawn from, or adverse comment made about, the silence of an accused or the absence of evidence for an accused (with some very strict exceptions).

An accused is presumed to be innocent unless and until there is a conviction at the end of the trial. Throughout the trial the prosecution bears the burden (or onus) of proving the case to the standard known as beyond reasonable doubt. Therefore at trial the prosecution, faced with a plea of not guilty, will have to call (in most cases) all witnesses able to give relevant evidence and the defence will be able to challenge that evidence by cross-examination and by its own evidence (if any). The jury's task (or the judge's, if it is trial by judge alone — available at the request of the accused and, in New South Wales and some other places, with the consent of the prosecution) is to determine the facts from that evidence and, taking into account the directions of law given by the judge, to decide whether or not the facts proved have established all the elements of the offence beyond reasonable doubt. While it is for the jury to find the facts and decide on a verdict, it must do so by applying the law. The judge directs the jury about the law and also summarises the cases of the prosecution and defence for them as shown by the evidence.

If at the end of the prosecution case the judge is of the

view that there could not be a conviction on the evidence available — that the jury could not reasonably and in accordance with law be satisfied of guilt beyond reasonable doubt — the judge may direct the jury to return a verdict of not guilty. That is another test that applies during the trial process — another gateway that has to be negotiated. Such a directed verdict cannot be appealed by the Crown in New South Wales and some other jurisdictions, but in some places (for example, Tasmania and Western Australia) it can.

The judge may also, at any time during the trial, invite the jury to end the trial there and then by returning a verdict of not guilty. (There cannot be an invitation to convict.) This is called a 'Prasad' direction to the jury (after the name of a case in which its availability was confirmed). It is yet another test applicable by the trial judge by which the prosecution case may be evaluated and disposed of — another gateway to be passed through.

The verdict in a trial (or in a summary hearing in the Local Court) can only be 'guilty' or 'not guilty' — and the test for a guilty verdict is satisfaction by all the jurors of proof beyond reasonable doubt. We do not have, as the Scots do, a verdict of 'not proven'. Therefore courts can only decide guilt. They do not make findings of innocence. If a case is not proved to the required standard then the verdict is not guilty; but that is not the same as innocent — the court makes no declaration of innocence.

Radio 'entertainer' Alan Jones, for instance, has been known to say that Sir Joh Bjelke-Petersen was 'found innocent' at his trial in Queensland in 1991. No such thing occurred. Indeed, the jury in that case failed to agree on any verdict, so Sir Joh was even further from any favourable result. A not guilty verdict simply means that the accused has not had the offence against him or her proved beyond reasonable doubt. He or she therefore continues to enjoy the presumption of innocence with which he or she started the trial; but there has been no decision on the question — no positive finding of innocence. A jury verdict (guilty or not guilty) in New South Wales must be by unanimous decision of the jurors. (In some other jurisdictions there can be majority verdicts in some circumstances.) In New South Wales guilty verdicts are given in almost 50 per cent of cases that go to trial; but the vast majority of all criminal cases — over 95 per cent — are disposed of by pleas of guilty at some stage of the proceedings and do not go to trial.

Judges in trials regulate the proceedings, make decisions on the admissibility of evidence, give directions of law and sum up the prosecution and defence cases for the jury. They may comment about the case in the course of summing up, but if they do they must make it clear to the jury that it is only a comment, able to be accepted or rejected by the jury. It is for the jury to decide the outcome. Judges are not able to comment about cases outside the court or the actual conduct of a trial for the reasons already explained in relation to magistrates.

PUNISHMENT

It is the judge's or magistrate's task to sentence a convicted person. This is done in a separate part of the trial following a guilty verdict (or in a hearing after a plea of guilty). Ordinarily Parliament will have prescribed a maximum penalty available to be imposed. The judge must set the penalty within the range of (effectively) nothing up to that maximum. By law, the maximum is reserved for offences that may be described as being in the worst class of cases of that particular offence, but not necessarily the worst imaginable cases.

To assist in that difficult task, judges have available to them the pronouncements of higher courts — guides, in effect, for the determination of proper sentences within the available ranges — and sentences imposed by other judges for similar offences. In a few categories of crime they are now assisted by sentencing guideline judgments, which are discussed in Chapter 8 Sentencing.

Judges are also assisted in gauging an appropriate community response to the crime by circumstances; by the fact that they live in the real world, have families and friends, cars and mortgages, pay tax, read newspapers, listen to the radio, watch television, travel on buses and trains, go to sporting events and mix professionally and socially with people from a wide range of occupations and backgrounds. They also host a procession of people of all descriptions and from all walks of life through their courts every working day. They also talk amongst themselves about appropriate ways in which to decide cases and keep watch on trends and attitudes within and outside their own jurisdictions. If judges once lived in ivory towers, not many do so now — despite the unthinking assertions of talkback.

Judges (and other judicial officers) are more accountable than any other public officials. Because they conduct their proceedings in public (with very few and limited exceptions) anybody can go in to observe and then report on what they have seen and heard. Judges and magistrates work under the constant public gaze. They give published reasons for their decisions. Except for the seven Justices of the High

Court (the ultimate court of appeal for Australia), in most cases they are subject to scrutiny and review by higher courts on appeal.

APPEAL

A convicted person may appeal against conviction and/or sentence. The Crown (or prosecution) in New South Wales cannot appeal against an acquittal. It can appeal (through the DPP) against the leniency of a sentence, but the test it must meet is that of manifest inadequacy: it must be able to show that the sentence was so light as to be clearly wrong or that some material error of fact or law was made by the sentencing judge (and evident from the remarks on sentence). It is not enough that the sentence may just be regarded as lenient. Even if it is accepted as manifestly inadequate, a superior court may not alter the sentence in the exercise of discretion that it quite properly retains for the purpose of doing justice in all the circumstances of the case.

CONCLUSION

It can be seen, therefore, that the process of criminal justice through the gateways described is far from a joke. But it is also not like the operation of a computer program or a multiple-choice, tick-the-boxes, type of exercise. It is a careful and measured progress. Judgment and discretion are required at virtually all stages from a number of different operatives; and whenever judgment or discretion is exercised there will be room for differing views. In this system the views of the decision makers and the reasons for their decisions are publicly known.

No other acceptable system has yet been shown to work for our conditions. We have not been able to devise any better system to serve the needs of a community characterised by great diversity and a strong preference for a high degree of personal freedom. As Winston Churchill might have said, it is not perfect — but it is better than all the other systems we have tried.

A system where judgment and discretion are applied under the glare of the public spotlight, while not operating with the precision and certainty of a computer program, is also very different from the kind of system often portrayed by the talkback 'entertainers'. Depending on the whim of the moment, they will tell you that the police do not have enough power — or that they have too much; that the lawyers are manipulating the system (for their clients or themselves); that magistrates and judges are ignoring the law, being too soft — or being unreasonably harsh; that not enough criminals are going to prison for long enough — or that too many of them are being treated brutally in oppressive conditions in gaols; that the penalties prescribed by law are too soft. They have whinges for all occasions and they are not consistent. They blow where the money is to be made.

If these 'opinion makers' were left just to clog the airwaves with gripes it would be one thing. Radios can be turned off. The damage is done, however, when a feedback loop forms between their uninformed rantings and the slogans of politicians — when the two groups encourage each other to believe that they are right — that the people are behind them — that they have answers to problems that they barely understand — and that they support each other in whatever spur-of-the-moment plans they conceive. Supported by the manipulations of the 'entertainers' the politicians then move to action — they change laws.

Our criminal justice system has been in operation for a very long time. It has withstood many tests, since long before talkback was invented. It has been subject to constant change and improvement, driven by the experience of those who work in it and who detect shortcomings that need correction. It is not perfect. No system devised by humans and created by the democratic political process, that depends on human input to address human behaviour, can be perfect. But it is a good deal better than talkback radio would have you believe.

Two: Policing Crime

A policeman's lot is not a happy one.

W. S. GILBERT
Barrister, lyricist and writer

Crime is committed when someone with the *motive* (or desire or inclination) and *opportunity* to do something that is against the criminal law is not under sufficient *control* to prevent it happening. That control may come from the individual's own strengths or it may come from restrictions imposed by others on the person's conduct. When crime happens the 'undertakers' — the police, prosecutors, courts and prisons — move in to deal with the consequences. Motive and opportunity arise often enough. The undertakers can have little, if any, effect on them. So it is on the control, or prevention, of crime that they should concentrate.

Crime has fashions. Those fashions are determined by social circumstances. However, crimes of personal violence and greed in one form or another happen all the time — essential human nature changes very little and only slowly.

To talk about an increase or decrease in crime without looking at the different types of crime and where and when they are being committed is misleading. The levels of offending in different categories of crime will vary at different times and in different places. Usually the rates of one or more types of crime will be rising slightly while the rates of others will be falling. There will usually be variations from place to place caused by local factors. How we interpret the statistics may depend to some extent on categorisation (how we describe the crimes — by reference to what ingredients) which may change over time for particular offences, on the source of the statistics (I have a deep distrust of them when produced by some parties), and on the use to which the publisher is attempting to put them.

'Lies, damn lies — and statistics', said Benjamin Disraeli, and that applies to crime statistics as well. They must be handled with care. An impression is instantly made when some startling figure is thrown out to the public, but it should always be examined carefully to see just what it really measures and what conclusions we can properly draw from it. For example, the number of crimes of a particular type may be higher now (say 3000 per year) than it was five years ago (say 1000 per year). Without more information, we might think that things are getting worse. But it might be that the figure has been dropping steadily since two years ago when the figure was 5000. That might in turn show that the policies adopted over the last two years are working. A political party in opposition might latch onto the first figures, but a party that has been in government for at least two years might emphasise the second set (especially if the 5000 figure were reached when the now-opposition party was in power!).

Elections cause crime waves. They must — just listen to the candidates! For months before elections it becomes unsafe to leave your homes — or even to stay in them. We could obviously go a long way towards reducing crime by not having elections. Alternatively, we could achieve the same result by having lots of elections because once the election is over, the crime wave miraculously disappears.

Between elections and in reality, of course, crime rates constantly fluctuate. If there is more crime, the policy makers (including the politicians) blame factors that they say they cannot control. They blame the breakdown of the family, the ineffectiveness of educational institutions, the declining influence of the churches, demographic changes, a general decline of morality, and so on. (They may be right, of course — and they should not be rinsing their hands of those problems. There may be something they can do about all this if they are prepared to put in the effort and wait for the results.)

But if crime rates fall, politicians immediately claim the credit, saying the fall is the result of the short-term policies they have been pursuing — usually more police, longer sentences, zero tolerance policing and so on.

But Politicians can get it wrong — and this can be proved. In the months leading up to the March 1999 NSW election there was much hysterical talk on both sides about mounting crime, about increasing crime rates, and (from the Opposition) about the ineffectiveness of present policies in curtailing crime. Barely three months later, in June 1999, the Bureau of Crime Statistics and Research (a part of the Attorney General's Department) published the results of research that it had been carrying out on crime trends in NSW in the period July 1997 to June 1999 — a two-year period including about 20 months before the election.

The Bureau reported that in their list of 16 offence categories over the period there was none that showed statistically significant upward trends in the monthly numbers of recorded criminal incidents. Downward trends were found in four categories (sexual assault, indecent assault and other sexual offences, robbery with a firearm, and motor vehicle theft). There was no trend either way in the numbers for the other categories. So there was no increasing crime rate. Where were the politicians getting their information?

Competent researchers (like the Bureau) adopt a different approach from politicians. They acknowledge that policy can make a difference in some cases, but the difference depends upon existing crime levels and trends which can happen quite independently of policy. Policies can help to push a trend along, but only by interacting with other factors 'on the ground'. So it is sterile and futile to just trot out the same old short-term policy mantras at every election. Myths.

POLICE AND POLICING

An excess of law inescapably weakens the rule of law.
LAURENCE H. TRIBE

One of the myths trotted out is that crime is reduced by employing more police — more police equals less crime. No: we would only see that effect if we had honest and competent police officers on every street corner and in every home, office, shop, pub and sporting venue. Numbers of police *do not* move up and down with the rate of crime, as many studies have shown. *The use to which police are put* does correlate with less crime, however. It is the fear of detection that has the greatest long-term policing effect on offending — by deterring it from happening in the first place. Intelligence-led, targeted policing can reduce crime.

The police don't always get it right, of course. Every

holiday period police stack the highways with hidden speed detectors and write thousands of tickets. The priority is clearly revenue raising. If it were crime reduction, the effort would be put into making these measures as visible as possible, with clearly marked cars everywhere and roadside stations displayed for all to see. Police would be stopping and speaking to offenders, not sending bills out in the mail: a kind of 'user pays' for lawbreaking, or a tax on offending. Motorists who are inclined to break the law need to be reminded constantly of the risk — they soon forget (or take the risk) if traps are hidden. And if they are caught in one, they just write a cheque to dispose of the problem. Deterrence, rather than imposition of penalty after the event, should be the general priority.

One of the explanations tentatively put forward for the fall noted in the Bureau of Crime Statistics' figures quoted above is that police had made a deliberate policy to target repeat offenders — people who had offended already more than once and were likely to offend again. If they could be identified and monitored in such a way as to discourage them from reoffending, or at least to enable quick arrests, crimes could be contained. The keys to such success are good training and equipping and expert advice and implementation. An appropriate range of police powers is also important, but a balance must be struck between those powers and individual freedoms. Even people who have broken the law in the past and paid the penalty are entitled to the ordinary rights that we all enjoy.

I have referred in passing to *zero tolerance policing*. It appeals most strongly to those unusual people who seem to be capable of zero tolerance in many things. But what does it mean?

Its origin was in the example of the 'broken windows' used in a 1982 magazine article in the United States. It argued that, just as a broken window left unmended was a sign that nobody cared for the building, which led to further property damage, so any disorder in the community sent a signal that nobody cared for the community and produced fear in the populace, serious crime and the 'downward spiral of urban decay'. Notwithstanding the leaps in logic involved, the message taken up from the article was that minor offences can have serious consequences for the community, so minor offences should be hit hard — with zero tolerance. A man named William Bratton became Chief of the Transit Police Department of New York City in 1990. He set about cleaning up the subway — restoring and maintaining order in a system that had fallen into decay and had become dangerous and unpleasant. Mr Bratton had a lot of quick success in the subway and moved above ground to be appointed New York's Police Commissioner in 1994. He had a lot of success there, too, but it would be quite wrong to say that he achieved it by fixing the broken windows. That would be to sell him short by a very large amount. Cleaning up a subway is one thing, improving law and order in a huge and complex city is quite another. His was as much a multi-pronged attack on the police force itself, as it was an attack on disorder in the streets. Indeed, he needed no more police or police powers to do a better job; he just made the existing system work more effectively.

His successor continued the policy, but narrowed it substantially to real zero tolerance under the urging of New York Mayor Giuliani (and his 'quality of life' campaign). Ultimately there was rebellion on the streets by citizens and the police against this unthinking form of policing. The president of the police union said: 'If we don't strike a balance between aggressive enforcement and common sense, it becomes a blueprint for a police state and tyranny.'

Zero tolerance policing means, for most legal professionals, something akin to total law enforcement — every minor infraction is punished to the full extent of the law. In New York, police were sent out to aggressively pursue even the most minor offences (like jaywalking, drinking in public, loitering, riding bicycles on footpaths etc.). The idea seems to be based also in part on the theory of selective incapacitation: that is, if you 'take out' particular minor offenders they will not progress to committing major offences (a similar theory to that underlying mandatory sentencing of the 'three strikes' variety). It is a seriously flawed theory. It also has the consequence, like mandatory sentencing, that minor offenders are sent to institutions where they soon learn to become major ones.

Another justification sometimes put forward for this sort of policing is that in the process of apprehending minor offenders, police may come across some who have committed major offences — a sort of by-product of police action that saves the time and effort of proper investigation.

In practice — and this is supported by studies from places where it has been tried, even New York — the result of zero tolerance policing is that scarce police resources are diverted from the investigation of serious crime (which carries on largely unimpeded) into the punishment without discretion of minor street and other offences. Police become bound to the work involved in processing huge numbers of petty offences. Citizens grow to despise police and regard themselves as living in a repressive society. There is no statistical support for its effectiveness outside a closed environment like a subway. In most places it is regarded as an interesting experiment that may have made some small contribution to an improvement in general order, but at a huge and unwelcome cost. The Australian politicians who went to New York (almost in procession) or who listened rapt to the ambassadors who visited Australia and became advocates of zero tolerance policing were, as in so many things, some distance behind the game. Support for zero tolerance seems to come from those with exactly the same level of knowledge about policing — zero!

Inspector David Darcy of the NSW Police Service wrote in 1999 in *Current Issues in Criminal Justice* that the term 'zero tolerance' when used in NSW means something different. He said that it should be viewed as 'no more than simply a catchy product name with little resemblance to its "New York cousin"'. He distinguished the New York policing environment from its Australian counterpart and noted that astute police managers here have quickly realised how questionable the implementation of the New York form of zero tolerance would be. In reality, street policing in NSW has become more focused on 'chasing and catching crooks, with large scale, tightly scripted, high profile policing operations addressing street violence and disorder' and focusing on crime hot spots. This is not zero tolerance policing — quite the reverse: police are given wide discretion to deal expeditiously and informally with minor offences and to move on quickly to prevent or deal with more serious crimes.

A senior lecturer at the NSW Police Academy — someone training police in this country — recently wrote about zero tolerance policing: 'We should carefully consider whether we really want a system that causes the law to over-reach and extend its net to enmesh many more people for non-serious matters ... The restriction of police discretion through the application of strict limitations, or even its total removal, can only lead to total law enforcement, a situation that is as unworkable as it is undesirable.'

Three: The Drug Problem

> *You do not examine legislation in the light*
> *of the benefits it will convey if properly*
> *administered, but in the light of the wrongs*
> *it would do and the harms it would cause if*
> *improperly administered.*
>
> LYNDON B. JOHNSON

> *Prescription heroin would save a heck of a*
> *lot of lives and would reduce other crime*
> *problems dramatically.*
>
> (RETIRED) DETECTIVE CHIEF INSPECTOR JOHN McKOY
> Former head of the Victorian Drug Squad

The criminal justice system, obviously enough, is concerned with the problem of illegal drugs — a problem that the Australian Bureau of Criminal Intelligence reports may cost Australia as much as $18 billion a year. Other systems are left to deal with the consequences of our most dangerous but legal drug, tobacco, the second most harmful, alcohol, and legal therapeutic drugs, largely without the intervention of the criminal law. So do illegal drugs deserve the attention we give to them at the expense of efforts we should be making to discourage the use of legal drugs? And does that attention stem more from the fact that they have been officially demonised than from any rational efforts to deal with them effectively?

Tobacco is the primary cause in Australia of premature and preventable death and disease. It is responsible for 80 per cent of drug-related deaths — up to about 19 000 each year. That number, fortunately, is beginning to fall (but take-up rates for tobacco use are not falling among women and young people). In the early 1960s nearly 60 per cent of Australian men smoked, now it is about 20 per cent. But tobacco's annual economic cost to Australia — including health care (800 000 hospital bed days per year) and loss of productivity in the workplace — is still about $13 billion (almost as much as the $15 billion brought in by international tourism). Governments gather only about $4 billion from taxes on tobacco. Alcohol is responsible for about 3600 deaths each year and a high level of disease and social disruption. Its economic cost to Australia (including alcohol-related accidents) is about $5 billion per annum. The abuse of therapeutic drugs (e.g. tranquillisers, analgesics) also brings a high social cost, much of which cannot be measured in dollar terms.

Illegal drugs — the ones the criminal law is required to deal with — account for only 3 per cent of preventable drug-related deaths: about 700 in Australia in 1999. Their economic cost to Australia, including property crime and law enforcement, is less than $2 billion per annum.

Yes, illegal drugs are a problem. Their use is often unpleasant and usually destructive and it brings unattractive and unwanted behaviours. But let us keep them in perspective. Let us not encourage the witch-hunts conducted by talkback and tabloids with their vested interests in looking at the world in black and white. Stories about goodness do not sell, except in churches and at award ceremonies.

Stories about evil are lapped up. They are easy sensational fodder for talkback. And nasty drug stories are open to the stroking of other latent prejudices and fears. Illegal drugs are sold by people of all ethnic backgrounds. There are some people of Vietnamese origin doing it in Sydney's Cabramatta — hardly surprising when people of Vietnamese origin make up a sizeable part of the population of that area. But this opens the door to demonising all people of Vietnamese origin as drug dealers.

The same applies to the linking of any other group to drugs. 'Race' is largely irrelevant to meaningful discussion of the drug problem itself. Focusing attention on race only makes it more difficult to formulate effective policies to deal with drugs, which affect all ethnic groups indiscriminately.

THE PROBLEM

What is the drug problem? It is different things to different people, so there is not likely to be just one way to 'fix' it — if that is possible at all.

Since man and woman first stood upright (and possibly even earlier) we have used drugs: things that grew or fermented in the first place, and then substances that were compounded. We have done so, at least to begin with, because we liked them. It is said that there is no accounting for taste — there is no controlling or legislating for it, either. Different people will go to different lengths to get things that they want. Some people become addicted to them. There will always be a demand for mood altering drugs, and there will always be a supply of them. So whether we like it or not, let us accept those as facts and work from there. We must be realistic. There is nothing wrong with wishful thinking and we should use it to set goals, but many goals will be unattainable in practice and we must accept that too. Life is about compromises and experience should guide us to acceptable ones in a rational manner.

Some members of communities, maybe even majorities, have taken the view from time to time that the consumption of a particular drug is a bad thing. They have attempted to prohibit people demanding drugs and people supplying them. A hundred years ago it was illegal to sell cigarettes in 14 of the United States of America, heroin was an ingredient in cough syrup and cocaine was in Coca-Cola. A couple of decades later alcohol was to be prohibited (along with heroin and cocaine — cigarettes were given a reprieve). Prohibition is the genesis of the modern drug problem, just as it has created problems, rather than solved them, in relation to other drugs in the past, as fashions have changed. The United States spends about $115 billion every year trying to enforce drug prohibition and it encourages its friends to follow the same line.

Prohibition of a marketable commodity for which there is a demand inevitably produces a black (or illicit) market. Black-market commodities sell at inflated markups (consider Robin Williams' 'Cocaine is God's way of saying you're making too much money'!). Large profits are generated by successful traders, the profits growing as one moves up the distribution tree. That is the nub of the drug problem, as I see it.

If expensive commodities are demanded by people unable to afford them with their own resources, they may use other people's resources. In connection with drugs, private property is simply stolen and converted into criminal profits.

The buyers are desperate. For the most part (although not exclusively) they are undisciplined addicts whose only concern in life is the next dose. They will do whatever they can to get it. It becomes the sole and immediate focus of all their attention and energies until (usually after about ten years, if they are still alive) they make the decision to stop. They prostitute themselves to finance it. They buy more to sell and finance their own use. They steal private property. Worldwide nearly $2 trillion a year is earned from the sale of heroin — that's a lot of handbags, videorecorders and bank holdups. The illegal drug trade is the third largest international industry after oil and arms.

The sellers are also highly anxious. Apart from those who deal to finance their own addiction, many have outlaid funds or gone into debt to obtain their supply. They must sell in order to pass on the ever-increasing profit margin further up the line where it is reinvested in further illegal activity.

Buyers and sellers need to be able to find each other, so centres become magnets for them — marketplaces. Why particular centres (Kings Cross and Cabramatta in Sydney, St Kilda and Footscray in Melbourne, Fortitude Valley in Brisbane and other centres in other places) develop in this way may be a matter for speculation, but it is known from experience that a crackdown on one merely displaces the market to somewhere else.

If people are required, because of legal prohibition, to introduce substances into their bodies in unhealthy conditions, disease will spread: blood-borne diseases such as hepatitis and HIV/AIDS. That is also a problem.

SCOPE OF THE PROBLEM IN AUSTRALIA

For the year 1998–99, according to the Australian Bureau of Criminal Intelligence, Australian Customs seized:

- 508 kilograms of heroin (up from 138 kilograms the previous year). A further 214 kilograms (up from 161) were seized by law enforcement agencies within Australia, making a total of 722 kilograms.
- 292 kilograms of cocaine (up from 78).
- 89 kilograms of ecstasy (up from 31 kilograms).
- 10 kilograms of amphetamines (down from 20 kilograms); and
- 47 kilograms of cannabis (up from 38).

Let us consider heroin for a moment. It is estimated that there are over 100 000 (perhaps as many as 300 000) heroin users of all ages in Australia, spending over $10 billion a year on about 10 tonnes of it (i.e. 10 000 kg). In one year only 722 kilograms were seized, less than 7 per cent of the total imported. It sells for as little as $20 a hit. It is plentiful and it is pure. More and younger people are using it.

CAN WE FIX IT?

The approaches we have been adopting for decades are based on wishful thinking and wilful blindness. They are based on a policy of prohibition, peddled by the United States. There needs to be a solid injection of reality, a recognition of human nature and what is practically achievable — and desirable — in this area. Illicit drugs are prohibited, but they cannot be eliminated. We must acknowledge that basic fact.

Australia's official strategy is directed at three Rs (reductions):

- *Supply reduction*, that is disrupting the importation, growth, production and supply of illicit drugs. The measures adopted include patrols of our border by sea and air; searches of incoming vessels, cargo and passengers and postal items; the detection of cannabis plantations and amphetamine factories; and the investigation of drug suppliers at all levels.

- *Demand reduction*, that is preventing and discouraging drug use, persuading and deterring people from seeking out supplies of drugs. Measures directed to these ends include education programs in schools and the community; deterrence through criminal penalties; treatment and rehabilitation programs for drug users (including abstinence-oriented strategies); and various support programs for those seeking to avoid or cease drug use.

- *Harm reduction (originally — 15 years ago — harm minimisation)*, that is reducing the impacts of drug-related harm on individuals and communities. Under this strategy come treatment and rehabilitation programs; needle and syringe programs; methadone maintenance programs; and, possibly, safe injecting premises.

The programs in place in each category are too numerous to detail here. Some are more effective than others. For example, saturation policing of one distribution centre as a supply reduction strategy has been tried. It may have worked for a time for that centre (satisfying the NIMBYs — 'not in my backyard') but it only displaced the problem to somewhere else. Customs seizures of heroin have increased in recent times, but they have not affected price, supply or purity. The only rational inference is that more heroin is being seized because more heroin is being sent here. It is simply not possible to search the 7 million shipping containers and 2 million airline passengers that arrive here each year (or all the airfreight and postal items) or to patrol every kilometre of our huge coastline and investigate every suspicious craft. How can we keep drugs out of the country if we cannot even keep them out of maximum security prisons?

Our harm reduction strategies have certainly been successful in containing HIV and other blood-borne diseases.

In the criminal law it is often suggested that Parliament and the courts should get tough on drugs and crime generally. There are two things to be said about that: first, they are tough; and secondly, being tough is no answer, anyway.

In relation to the first of these responses, the NSW Bureau of Crime Statistics and Research has reported that since 1990 the average length of prison sentences has increased and more sentences (as opposed to non-custodial penalties) have been imposed in most categories of serious crime. The prison population has been rising steadily in New South Wales since 1990. It rose 11 per cent in 1998 to over 7000 and continued to rise throughout 1999 and 2000. So any perception that the law generally is going soft is erroneous by that measure.

Research also shows that increasing penalties, particularly for drug-related crime, has no demonstrable effect on offending. Drug users do not stop to consider the possible criminal justice consequences of their acts. Indeed, to understand their motivation think about tobacco smokers. Tobacco contains nicotine. Nicotine is an addictive drug. Users want more of it. Their ability to choose *not* to use it is significantly impaired by that addiction. The tobacco companies know that; they seek to maintain and increase their profits by enlisting more addicts in new categories and at younger ages. Youth are also attracted to heroin — by the excitement and glamour popularly associated with it, by exposure, peer pressure, experimentation and a curiosity often born of boredom and alienation. They may become addicts. Then they want more of it. Their ability to choose to say no is also significantly impaired by that addiction and by the social influences operating all around. (So much for the 'just say no' idea.) A person acting without a free choice is unlikely to think much about the consequences of that action.

Drug suppliers do not expect to get caught. The ones high up the tree, for whom the possible penalties are greatest, do not even expect to be identified, let alone charged. They are career criminals, pursuing profit by involvement in a distant market — profit that can be recycled into further criminal ventures.

We can selectively lock away people for longer, as the figures seem to indicate we are doing. But imprisonment, generally speaking, just makes bad people worse. It opens up criminal opportunities for other bad people who have not been apprehended.

WHAT WE SHOULD DO

I do have a suggestion as to what we should do, at least in relation to heroin. It is not a completely new idea. Many people have written and spoken on the issue from similar points of view. I do not say it is the answer, but I do say that it should be considered, discussed and evaluated. It might also contain the seeds of answers to the problems of other drugs as well as heroin. It is a combination of prohibition and strict regulation, but with an injection of reality.

The connection between heroin use and crime must be weakened, if not broken. The only effective way of doing that is to reduce, if not eliminate, the profits generated by the trade. In part, this is an economic argument; thirst for money motivates most criminals.

Make heroin available free to addicted users on prescription by licensed medical practitioners. This is not heroin on demand, available from the corner store. This measure addresses the needs of those who presently prostitute themselves, steal or find other buyers in order to buy unknown substances to inject into their veins in unsanitary conditions. It would be a safety valve, for use when earlier influences have failed.

This need not be an expensive solution. It costs less than $1 to make a dose of heroin. And Australia is in a good position to do this. Australia grows opium poppies under controlled conditions in Tasmania. We supply nearly half of the world's legitimate opioids for medical use. There is certainly scope for the crop to be increased. Consideration is being given to growing it elsewhere in Australia. License growers, importers (if necessary to make up quantities), manufacturers and suppliers of heroin. Pharmaceutical drug companies, for example, could tender for the production work which would be carried out under strict controls.

Australia is an island and we should take advantage of that feature (as we presently do in a number of ways). Unlike most countries we can control to some extent the flow of goods and people across our border (although, as I have noted, there is a limit to what we can achieve against determined adversaries). It is rational, therefore, to maintain prohibition on the importation (and exportation) of heroin and to continue to enforce the criminal sanctions that apply to unauthorised activity. Possession and supply that is also unauthorised (i.e. not for the purposes of addicted users) should also be criminal. Unauthorised activity will still occur; but if it is not so profitable it will diminish and be more easily policed.

Would there be a honeypot effect — the attraction of addicts from other places? That can be addressed by imposing a residential qualification on prescription and by enforcing the laws against the immigration of drug addicts.

Would it encourage a boom in heroin use? First-time users would still obtain heroin from the black market. But the profit for the suppliers would shrink — their regular money comes from addicts, not from experimenters (indeed, first doses are sometimes given away with an eye to future profits). Amounts required for sale on the street would fall. Prices on the street may rise because the distributors would need to cover high costs from smaller sales — a further disincentive to the reduced number of buyers. Alternatively, if supplies are at a high level and demand is low, prices may fall. Either way it doesn't matter, the illegal market would shrink because regular users would get their heroin free.

With the addicts being attended to in a medical environment, the perverse glamour of unregulated heroin use would diminish. Addicted users would be exposed to proper health and treatment programs, social support and other rehabilitative services (but should not be forced to undergo treatment as a condition of getting heroin). Educational programs directed at abstinence should be continued and expanded at all levels of society. The message would continue to be that drug use is undesirable and can be dangerous, but addicts would be kept alive, comparatively healthy and useful until they chose to take a different path.

A regime of this sort would make heroin use an unglamorous health and social issue. It would shrink the black market.

It would ensure for addicts measured doses, purity and safe ingestion, reducing further the risk of blood-borne diseases like hepatitis and HIV/AIDS. It would clean up our streets, by and large, and substantially reduce criminal offending to support addiction.

The question is often asked in shrill desperation: *'But what sort of message would this send to the community, particularly the young?'* There are two answers to that.

First, the content of a message can be manipulated by those sending it. Politicians know that through the media action can be 'sold' to the public in many different ways. Spin doctors abound. The message that is sent can be the message that is intended to be sent.

Secondly, the message intended to be sent should be that those in charge have recognised that we have a problem, that they want to fix it and that they want to do so in a responsible, sensible and effective way, if they can, without empty posturing and the wasted expenditure of millions of dollars of public funds on ineffective action. The message can be that drug use is a health and social issue to be addressed in those quarters — that drug users are not demons but are people with all the weaknesses and strengths of other people who for the moment need help and support to change their habits. The message is that there is no glamour in drug use, that it is harmful and that steps can be taken to reduce and prevent that harm. Finally, the overall message that should be crafted and sent is that all drug use is undesirable and that there are very good reasons for not commencing; but that we want to keep alive those who have, so that they can stop.

Once a regime of this sort for heroin is found (through scientific trials) to produce benefits it might be possible to consider taking a final — bold — step. We have demonstrated a little success in turning around the harm caused by tobacco and alcohol. (A great deal more could be done if governments could reduce their dependence on the tax revenue the markets produce.) The prohibition of alcohol has been tried in western society and has failed. Regulation is preferable.

To eliminate the generation of criminal profits from all dealing in prohibited drugs the prohibitions themselves may be reduced to a practical level in a measured way, with strong controls being put in place at the same time to protect minors and maintain public health and order. While there might be a slight short-term increase in consumption, we might be able to achieve at least the modest measures of success we have had in relation to tobacco and alcohol. This would be a policy of openness and confrontation: getting the problem out in the open and confronting it together. The market might then find its own level through regulation, which could be productive of much less harm than the present arrangements.

WHAT ELSE WE SHOULD DO

In the meantime there are less radical measures over a broad range of options that should be adopted immediately. They also concern heroin use.

• Methadone programs should be continued. There is overwhelming scientific evidence that methadone maintenance programs enable users to return to useful and productive lives until they are in a position to discontinue drug use altogether. It keeps them alive, reasonably healthy and away from your property.
• Needle and syringe distribution programs should be

continued and expanded. They have significantly contributed to Australia's noted success in containing HIV/AIDS and other blood-borne diseases.

- Safe injecting premises should be established, as recommended by the Police Royal Commission after detailed study in May 1997 and, a little more tentatively, by the NSW Drug Summit in May 1999. What is preferable: clean, regulated facilities or disorder and danger in the streets?

- A trial of medically prescribed heroin should be held. Trials have yielded valuable lessons elsewhere and we need to know if the medical prescription of heroin would produce similar benefits in our social circumstances. It may not be a solution by itself, but it may be part of one.

- Diversionary schemes (schemes that take the management of the problem out of the strict processes of the criminal courts and into the hands of other agencies in the community better able to deal with it) should be adopted to help break the nexus between addiction and repeat criminal offending. Drug-free treatment programs offered by non-government agencies should be publicly supported.

- Decriminalisation of cannabis, along the lines adopted in South Australia, the Australian Capital Territory and Victoria, should be implemented.

- It defies understanding that the self-administration of drugs should be a criminal offence. Isn't the user doing enough self-harm without having a criminal penalty loaded on top?

I acknowledge that there may be unresolved practical problems associated with these proposals, but they need to be explored in a rational and constructive way and without the present level of ideological disputation.

DRUG SUMMIT

What we are doing is not working and we have to try to find a better way. I firmly believe the government should try at least one safe injecting house and see how it goes.

(RETIRED) DETECTIVE CHIEF INSPECTOR JOHN MCKOY (AGAIN)

In May 1999 the NSW Government honoured an election promise (exceptionally) and held a Drug Summit over a period of one week. A national drug conference had been held by police and others earlier in the year in Adelaide, but this was the first serious effort by an Australian government to discover more about the problem from those affected by it and to apply that knowledge constructively. As such it was of great national significance and its outcomes are therefore important. On 21 May 1999 the government released a communique of 20 principles and 172 recommendations endorsed by the summit.

There was really only one 'courageous' decision (as Sir Humphrey Appleby of 'Yes, Minister' might have said) and that was to sanction a trial of a medically supervised injecting room. This was in recognition of the need to decrease over-dose deaths, provide a gateway to treatment and reduce the problems of discarded needles and users injecting in public places. The trial was to be undertaken by a local council or a non-government organisation.

A safe injecting room is only one tentative step, but a step in the right direction giving some faint hope of more rational policies in the future. To that extent, and for the good it is capable of doing, it is to be welcomed and encouraged. But doubts must linger about whether the proposal merely enabled the politicians to look as if they were actually doing something constructive — and did it not also have the benefit of perhaps easing in a small way the pressures on our over-crowded gaols and under-resourced hospitals?

We can do things to reduce the demand for drugs; but not eliminate it. We can do things to reduce their supply; but alone, that inflates criminal profits and increases the risk of harm to all concerned. We can do much more to reduce harm, but only by some constructive thought about workable solutions that accommodate unalterable reality — and human nature.

Four: Starting Young

I've been struck by the upside-down priorities of the juvenile justice system. We are willing to spend the least amount of money to keep a kid at home, more to put him in a foster home, and the most to institutionalise him.

MARIAN WRIGHT-EDELMAN

W. C. Fields said that anybody who hates children and dogs can't be all bad! Whatever that says about the late Mr Fields, it does not provide a recipe for dealing with children (or dogs). After all, some of our most famous people started life as children . . .

Children often act like children. They throw things (like rocks from road overpasses) to see what happens if they hit something. They use knives to see what they can achieve with them — perhaps something like they saw in a movie or simulated in a video game. They steal or act as drug dealers to get money to spend. The motivation for action is usually simple and direct — and childishly irresponsible. They then react like children to the results of their actions. However, if adults become involved — maybe as the butt of a child's actions — they often react as they would against another adult, not as they should against a child.

Let me set such a scene: if a twelve-year-old sprays graffiti on a wall, the owner of the wall will be angry and will seek compensation for the damage and punishment of the offender. That is a perfectly natural reaction at the individual level. But it will be taken up and magnified by the (adult) public media: that twelve-year-old will be portrayed as a lawless vandal and all sorts of retribution will be demanded against him and against all other children of that age who carry out anti-social acts of all kinds. That individual adult's anger and frustration will be generalised. A raft of measures will be demanded of the government to prevent such acts occurring in the future, everything from curfews to banning the sale of paint in spray cans. It will be demanded that police have the power to arrest and detain children doing certain things or having a certain appearance (and presumably punish them in some way, or at the very least take them home — if they have one to be taken to). The politicians will weigh in with demands for laws making it an offence for children to be together in public places, to wear their caps back-to-front, or to look different from adults (or something equally nebulous and fatuous).

This is a prime example of concentrating resources at the wrong end of a problem. And while graffiti damage is ugly and annoying, most people do not perceive it as a threat to society.

What sort of a juvenile problem are we concerned with? In 1997-98 in the whole of New South Wales 1117 criminal matters involving child offenders aged 10 to 14 years (almost all of them minor offences) were finalised in the courts (about 20 a week). With an increase in police cautioning and youth conferencing, a reduction of 15 per cent occurred in the following year. Hardly an epidemic of juvenile lawlessness.

Instead of reacting in panic we should be looking at the situation rationally like the adults we are supposed to be. Yes, as a first step in the graffiti case we should attend to the delinquent and sort out that immediate problem as best we can; but then let us ask that wonderful question that we so often forget to ask: 'why?' Why did the child spray the wall? Was it so that he could make his mark, show that he exists, establish a place in the world and a relevance for his own being? And was that because he was unable to do those things in 'normal', more socially acceptable, ways? Ways like demonstrating achievement to (and being acknowledged and supported by) his family, like passing exams at school, like being accepted in a sporting team or a social club or even a group of law-abiding peers doing lawful things in lawful places? Was it also because he saw it as OK to deface an object for which he had no respect? Was the wall an example of property — property in which he and his family could not share because of their fortunes in society, that was controlled by distant, privileged groups, property whose place in the grand scheme of things he could not appreciate? Was that because of his having missed out on a sympathetic education? Was it school property that he defaced (as occurs in 40 per cent of reported incidents of graffiti vandalism)?

When we think we have some answers to that question — why? — we should then be asking ourselves what we can do to prevent such behaviour in the future. What we can do to encourage children to want to stay at school (sorry, that might need some more money for education and special programs aimed at 'problem' children); to provide support for families in crisis or at risk of breakdown (sorry, more money again); to provide acceptable social outlets for the energy of youth (again, more money); and to provide desirable employment at which the young can aim (more money, or just the right ethos?).

In the meantime, it is fast, easy and cheap (for those who do it) to condemn offenders and to raise hysteria among the public — to frighten people into entrusting the all-wise and all-powerful government to solve the problem, while allowing the (adult) public to vent its frustrations with calls for retribution and revenge. The public then requires the criminal justice system to relieve those frustrations with action. Then it is no longer a cheap option simply to condemn.

CHILDREN IN THE LAW

For legal purposes, in our society all persons under the age of 18 years are children. The law makes a number of special provisions for them. There are some things they cannot do — they can't vote, they can't join the armed forces, they can't marry without permission, they can't be admitted to certain entertainments and premises. There are some special arrangements made in their favour, however — they must attend school until at least 15 years, they are entitled to support, if not by family then by the state (and in NSW they can ride their bicycles on the footpath).

In the criminal law there is a whole range of special provisions for dealing with children in special courts and institutions. They are treated under a regime that is very different from that applying to adults, the overriding objective being (at least in theory) to act in the best interests of the child. The goal is to set the child back on the straight and narrow path to a socially responsible and productive adulthood.

Unfortunately, however, many people who are legally children act in fact like adults — or at least, like some people over the age of 18 years. And it doesn't matter to a victim of crime how old the criminal may be, the crime has still been committed, with all its unhappy consequences. Such a victim may find it hard to accept that the criminal should be treated in a special fashion just because he or she has not reached the eighteenth birthday.

Such a victim might think that if a crime that could have been committed by an adult has been committed against him or her, then the criminal should be treated like an adult. Such a victim might think that is logical, but it is not. While the crime *could* have been committed by an adult, in fact it was not, and it is the criminal that requires attention, not the crime. The crime is over, but the criminal and the victim linger on.

The victim might be attracted to the way things have gone in the United States. In late 1999 the *Washington Post* reported:

> In 1999, 100 years after the establishment of the nation's first juvenile court in Cook County, Ill., virtually all states have succeeded in passing legislation to criminalize or 'adultify' their juvenile justice systems. It is now far easier to transfer juveniles to adult court, hold them in adult jails and sentence them to adult prisons. Most of the laws require judges to impose harsher and longer sentences than ever before.

But children are not just small adults.

There is a degree of arbitrariness in designating those under 18 years as children, but the line has to be drawn somewhere. It is not so long ago that it was drawn at 21. Why does it have to be drawn at all? Why should not all offenders against the criminal law be treated the same way, regardless of age? The reason is that children are children, even though some may mature into practical adulthood before turning 18. The physical and psychological maturing process continues throughout life but takes place most rapidly in the early years. It may be illustrative to consider Shakespeare's seven ages of man, but the boundaries of those divisions too are fuzzy. Some people progress from one to the next at earlier or later chronological ages than others. So it is with legal adulthood — some are ready for it before 18 and some after 18, but for practical purposes we have set 18 years as the boundary.

But even those under 18 are dealt with differently to take account of changes in physical and psychological development during that period, depending again (for practical reasons) on age divisions. Under 10 years a child cannot, by law, commit a crime; that is, cannot be dealt with under the criminal law for any conduct (even if, committed by an older person, it could clearly be regarded as criminal). It is conclusively presumed, as a matter of law, that such a person does not yet know that certain conduct is seriously wrong and morally reprehensible (as opposed to just mischievous, naughty or disobedient). Of course, there are other ways of dealing with 'problem children' of this age.

Between 10 and 14 years that presumption can be rebutted. That is, the child can be made liable to the criminal law if it can be proved by the prosecution that he or she did know that what was done was against the community's laws (and not just naughty behaviour). There is talk about reducing the upper limit from 14 to a lower age.

Between 14 and 18 this presumption (known as *doli incapax* — incapacity for guile or guilt) does not apply. The child is dealt with under the regime prescribed by the criminal law, but in a special court and subject to special procedures.

Furthermore, if a child (i.e. between 10 and 18 years) is to be dealt with for a serious offence, such as homicide, that child may be dealt with first by the Children's Court for the preliminary hearing but then 'at law', that is, in a normal 'adult' court with the ordinary rules applying. The procedures may be modified in a particular case to suit the people involved and any penalty imposed, of course, must take into account the age and circumstances of the child, the facilities available and the special principles that apply to dealing with children.

Children become adults, but they are not adults. Naughty children, even criminal children, act differently from adults, for different reasons and should be treated differently from adults if they are to have a chance of becoming good adults later on.

Adults know about rules. They know that society has set rules for the conduct of its members and that if they break those rules they should be punished. Children are learning about rules. They need rules too, just as adults do, but they need to learn them and to learn the consequences of not obeying them. They practise this themselves as they grow. Give a group of kids of a certain age a ball — any sort of ball — in a backyard or on a street or in a park and they will either play a game according to rules they already know or make up a new game to fit the circumstances. Listen to them setting the rules, and the penalties for breaking them. (Backyard cricket is a perfect example.)

CHILDREN AS OFFENDERS

In 1999 a boy was charged in New South Wales with manslaughter, the unlawful killing of another person. At the age of 10 he had pushed into the George's River a smaller and weaker, protesting boy aged six. The younger boy drowned.

This being a serious offence, it was determined that the boy (call him W) should be dealt with at law. The Chief Magistrate of the Children's Court heard committal proceedings against W in that court and found that, in his view, there was no reasonable prospect that a jury would convict. W was discharged.

In accordance with usual procedure that decision was reviewed by my Office, the NSW DPP. The law was considered along with the evidence available in the case. Advice was provided by lawyers who were involved in the case. I disagreed with the Chief Magistrate and took the view that it could not be said that there was no reasonable prospect of conviction by a reasonable jury properly instructed as to the law (the test to be applied in such circumstances). Clearly this was a matter on which reasonable minds could legitimately differ. It was certainly not, as one newspaper reported later, 'a public rebuttal of the Children's Court Chief Magistrate', nor was any 'public uproar' a factor in the decision.

W was tried for manslaughter in the Supreme Court, the highest state criminal court. That venue, rather than the District Court, was considered the more appropriate because of the exceptional nature of the proceedings and the special measures that would have to be taken during the trial. The case ran its full course. There was no directed verdict of acquittal, the jury was not invited by the judge to bring in an early verdict of not guilty. The jury retired on one day and delivered its not guilty verdict on the next, after full consideration.

The facts of what happened that day on the riverside were not really in dispute. The real issue was probably (and one can never say for certain what is in the minds of jurors) whether or not W, whose chronological age was 10 years at the time of the offence, but of whom evidence had been given that he was somewhat 'backward' in a number of respects, had been proven to have acted criminally — whether or not the presumption of *doli incapax* had been rebutted by the prosecution.

In the event, the jury acquitted and no criticism can be made of that outcome. That result could not have been known by me at the time the decision was made to prosecute (any more than it could have been known by the Chief Magistrate at the time of his decision) and it does not prove that he or I was right or wrong. The forecasting of the prospects of conviction must always be made on the basis of the material available at the time and an assessment of how a trial is likely to proceed. It is not a foregone conclusion. We have a system of trial by jury for serious cases. It is the jury that decides the result. If I am to decide the result, by not putting up for trial those cases that satisfy the tests to be applied, then the law will have to be changed.

W was an exceptional case and therefore prompted exceptional reactions. A Sydney QC was quoted, after the trial and acquittal, anonymously, as saying: 'Pushing ahead with this trial is a shift back to a vindictive, barbaric past, where children were as harshly punished as adults.' What a load of ignorant tripe! The facts were that a child to whom the criminal law applied killed another child in a way which, had he been an adult, would have been described as cold-blooded and callous. The law, its normal processes and all the established tests in place were applied. The accused was acquitted, as happens in a little over 50 per cent of trials that are run in New South Wales. He was not punished at all, let alone in the way in which adults are punished, nor would he have received adult punishment if he had been convicted.

A tract handed out on a suburban railway station during the trial was even more bizarre. It claimed that W, although an innocent child, was prosecuted only because the government was running a law and order agenda and the Attorney General had secretly signalled to me that W should be put on trial for political purposes, to show how tough the government could be!

While that was just more tripe as far as I was concerned, it was a potentially dangerous demonstration of the harm that can be done by 'law and order auctions', tough talk about the criminal law and the talkback line that crime is the government's fault and that it must therefore be seen to be doing something about it. The authors of the tract and their supporters wanted the recipients of the pamphlet to believe that the criminal justice process had been corrupted and perverted by a government keen to demonstrate its toughness on crime at any cost and using me as the instrument (which is the part that offends most of all!).

The wheel had turned full circle.

And potentially dangerous? Yes, because a campaign of that kind that reached the attention of a jury might well result in the aborting of a trial and all the financial and personal costs that would involve.

Children come in all shapes and sizes, from all kinds of backgrounds, with the full range of emotions and temptations. Some are loners, some hang out in groups. Some are bad, some are good; most are a bit of both in varying proportions at different times. Some tell lies, some don't. Some lie about certain matters, others lie about other things. One size certainly does not fit all, any more than it does for adults.

But the factors that influence criminal offending are there for all to see. If a child has educational problems and low self-esteem, he or she will have limited employment opportunities. There will be a feeling of powerlessness and of social isolation. That may lead to abuse of alcohol or other drugs and to seeking refuge in a delinquent peer group. Then comes criminal offending.

In New South Wales alone we are making new criminals at the rate of about one every two hours, day after day, night after night. How? The Bureau of Crime Statistics and Research tells us that each year in New South Wales there are about 20 000 notifications for child abuse and neglect. At least a quarter of those children will commit crimes. That is about 100 new offenders — and offences — each week, on top of those who are already adult and other regular offenders. True, many of those children will only offend once or twice, but many will progress through stages of petty offending to more serious offences, being exposed to drug use and drug-related crime as they go. If they are unlucky enough to be locked up on that first or second offence, they will learn in an institution how to reduce the risk of being caught the next time.

Unless something changes radically, the production line of criminals in Australia will continue to churn out offenders at an increasing rate.

Many adults in the community find it easier to treat all juveniles indiscriminately. When NSW Premier Bob Carr talked about groups of youths wearing baseball caps back to front he gave every citizen a means of identifying juvenile delinquents, rightly or wrongly. (Surely he was not talking about Lleyton Hewitt!) Laws have been passed without wide consultation — so far in operation only in a couple of country areas — that allow police to stop, question and round up children off the streets and return them to their homes (if they have one), even though they have not committed any offences. The theory seems to be that parents are responsible for juvenile offending and that it will not occur if the children are returned home. These laws will eventually be shown to be ineffective and undesirable demonstrations of simplistic and token 'toughness'.

Some people would like children to be treated as adults. There has been a call to 'get tough' and to name children publicly when they are brought before the courts. The only reason for such a demand can be a desire to expand whatever punishment might be imposed by the court more informally in the child's social environment. There is now the power in a court to order that the name of a child convicted of a serious offence — normally not allowed to be made known to the public at large — be published or broadcast if the judge is satisfied that it is in the interests of justice and that such prejudice as might be caused to the child does not outweigh those interests. One must ask what that might achieve in making the child a better adult. It is to be hoped that, given the tight conditions, orders are made only in cases where the defendants have most of the qualities of a legal adult.

A TIME FOR CHANGE?

One of the fascinations of the criminal law is that it never stands still. There is always something happening somewhere that sooner or later is going to make a difference to what we do. Another is that change can come from unexpected directions.

Sometimes it takes a while to happen. In February 1993

two ten-year-old boys lured a two-year-old boy named Jamie Bulger away from a shopping centre in Bootle, Merseyside, England. They took him to a railway track and battered him to death. They were found quickly enough, the early part of the abduction was recorded on the shopping centre's security cameras. They were dealt with following procedures that were much the same as those that applied to W in Sydney, their trial taking place the next year when they were 11. However, they were convicted of abduction and murder and eventually, under English procedures that are not the same as ours, ordered to be detained for a minimum of 15 years.

Various appeals and other proceedings followed; but the proceedings relevant to us here took place on 15 September 1999 in the European Court of Human Rights in Strasbourg, France, in the Grand Chamber presided over by 17 judges from 17 different countries. These proceedings were able to be brought because the United Kingdom is a party to the European Convention on Human Rights, and Britain's conduct is accountable to the standards of the Convention.

On 16 December 1999 the European Court delivered its judgment. Among its rulings it held that the defendants had not received a fair trial because they had not been able to participate effectively in their trial. The trial had taken place in an 'adult' court with all its formality over a period of three weeks and with a great deal of publicity. Special measures had been taken to modify the procedure to accommodate the defendants' young age. They were taken to see the courtroom in advance, the procedures that would be followed were explained to them, the hearing times were shortened so as not to tire them unduly. Nevertheless the formality and ritual of the court must have been incomprehensible and intimidating to a child of 11. They were seated in a specially raised area (so as to enable them to observe what happened), but that exposed them more prominently to others in the court. While the European Court held that they would have felt guilt, distress, anguish and fear, that was not enough by itself to have made the trial unfair. What the Court had to consider was whether the basic court procedures that are generally there to safeguard the rights of adults on trial (such as public access and reporting) should have been changed so as to create an environment that promoted the defendants' understanding and participation in the trial process.

The Court

> considered it essential that a child charged with an offence should be dealt with in a manner which took full account of his age, level of maturity and intellectual and emotional capacities, and that steps were taken to promote his ability to understand and to participate in the proceedings. In respect of a young child charged with a grave offence attracting high levels of media and public interest, this could mean that it would be necessary to conduct the hearing in private, so as to reduce as far as possible the child's feelings of intimidation and inhibition, or, where appropriate, to provide for only selected attendance rights and judicious reporting.

The two boys had been suffering from the psychological consequences of their crime. They had found the trial distressing and frightening and had not been able to concentrate during it or to discuss it with their lawyers. The Court

> did not consider that it was sufficient . . . that the applicants were represented by skilled and experienced lawyers . . . it was highly unlikely that either applicant would have felt sufficiently uninhibited, in the tense court room and under public scrutiny, to have consulted with them during the trial or, indeed, that, given their immaturity and disturbed emotional state, they would have been capable outside the court room of co-operating with

their lawyers and giving them information for the purposes of their defence.

The UK Government will have to respond to this judgment. How it does so will be a matter of great interest; but changes there must be to the procedures adopted when dealing with juvenile crime. The commencement of the operation of the European Convention will be significant.

Australian governments do not have to respond to it directly, but it would be very unwise of them not to do so in some fashion. At the heart of our criminal justice system is the notion of a fair trial, fair to both the accused and the community. If that cannot be obtained, then the proceedings cannot continue. Powerful and persuasive observations have been made by the European Court of Human Rights — not a body that can be ignored — on the need for special steps to be taken to ensure a fair trial for young offenders. They provide fuel for submissions that will no doubt be made to our courts and which may well persuade our judges that there has to be another way. Orders may be made that matters cannot proceed unless changes are put in place.

In the ordinary course of events our governments will probably follow behind and eventually respond to those rulings, but wouldn't it be nice if, just for once, they actually led reform and took action before such rulings became necessary?

CHILDREN AS VICTIMS AND WITNESSES

What the European Court of Human Rights has said about child defendants also applies, for obvious reasons, to child victims and witnesses in criminal proceedings.

Increasingly commonly, children come before the 'adult' criminal courts as victims of crime and as witnesses in proceedings against adults. For example, in the last decade particularly there has been the exposure of a long-term epidemic of child sexual abuse, which is still continuing. Most commonly there are allegations of misconduct in the family or immediate social context, but teachers, priests, scout leaders, music teachers etc. have been implicated. Certainly the modern environment is more conducive to the reporting of abuse. Children generally are better educated, more self-confident, better equipped to report wrongdoing against them and there is much greater awareness among teachers, health care professionals and others of the nature and extent of the problem. There are people, on the other hand, who claim that the modern environment leads to false reports being more readily made. Whatever the truth, the criminal justice system is left to find it.

Our system is not well equipped to cater for children. Even our courtrooms are completely inadequate. Often a child witness cannot be seen or heard (not even satisfying the old proverb about children) without taking special measures which themselves can be intimidating (perching a child in a prominent position or shoving a microphone in his or her face). Child victims are often confronted by their victimisers, although closed-circuit television is used in many courts to mitigate this impact. Unfortunately this has the consequence that the children often seem to the jury to be remote and detached while giving evidence and their reactions to questioning cannot be properly assessed. It is difficult to find the right balance between full confrontation and complete protection.

Countless reports and recommendations have been made

about the problems encountered and measures that might be taken to ameliorate them. Even the Royal Commission into the NSW Police Service made a number of recommendations about child witnesses. Little is done probably because of the need to coordinate action by all the agencies involved in any changes to the system and because of agency rivalries and the cost of change. Difficult problems are ignored in favour of addressing those with more immediate electoral dividends that are easier to solve. The reports gather dust on shelves and the recommendations are acknowledged in passing and then forgotten.

CHILD SEX ABUSE

In cases involving children as victims — usually of sexual abuse — the rate of conviction may be lower than average. There may be a number of reasons for this, but it has led some people to suggest that a completely different regime should be created to deal with such cases. Is it possible to throw out the bathwater and keep the baby?

What is the reaction of jurors in these cases? One juror in a NSW country town wrote to me about the experience, having come to the conclusion that all sexual assault cases — not only those involving children — should never be tried by juries. (The case in point, however, did involve a child victim of sexual assault.) The juror noted that for the majority of the jurors the victim was presumed guilty and had to prove her innocence. She was on trial — presumably because of the manner in which she was supposed to have acted — not the accused. Some jurors also reacted against the possibility that the girl might get victim's compensation. Eventually the juror who wrote had been persuaded to join the others in a not guilty verdict, just to end the matter.

Even if juries do their job properly, there are always special problems with these cases. Often the events took place some time ago. There may have been no complaint close to the time (perhaps, in truth, because the child was too frightened to complain). There may be no corroboration of the victim's evidence — offences of this kind are usually committed in private, where there are no witnesses. There may be no objective evidence (e.g. medical evidence) which supports the allegation. It may be a case of the victim's word against the word of the accused, who can call evidence of good character in support of the defence. It may be possible to show that the victim disliked the accused for other reasons (perhaps, in the case of a child, because of discipline handed out by the accused) and therefore wants to pay back; and so on.

Uncertainties of that kind may make any jury reluctant to accept the evidence of a victim to the standard of beyond reasonable doubt, knowing what the consequences can be for the accused. If that happens the consequences for the victim just have to be dealt with somewhere else.

Some of the various suggestions that have been made to change the system in abuse cases are as follows:

- that, as in some states in the United States, there should only be a prosecution if there is corroborative evidence available;
- that there should be trials by judge alone in child sexual assault cases;
- that there should be special tribunals established for offences involving children;

- that only the civil standard of proof should be required — on the balance of probabilities — making it easier to obtain convictions than in other criminal cases;
- that there should be no trial at all, but a system whereby the adult offender may admit the offence and be diverted into a treatment and social rehabilitation program to prevent future offending.

How much of a problem is sexual offending against children? Much of it goes unreported. Much of it, once reported, is unsubstantiated for one reason or another. However, in the five-year period 1991-92 to 1995-96 there were 25 941 cases of substantiated child sexual abuse reported in Australia, 15 968 (61.6 per cent or 3193 per year — more than eight a day) in New South Wales. But for that period in New South Wales an average of only 635 persons per year (i.e. in 20 per cent of cases) were charged in the criminal courts. Only 42 per cent (266 per year) pleaded guilty or were found guilty. The average conviction rate at trial (i.e. of those who did not plead guilty and who defended the allegations) was 34 per cent.

Researchers have drawn two conclusions from these figures. First, that the vast proportion of cases of child sexual abuse never get before the courts; and secondly, that the adversarial justice system is not very effective in dealing with the problem.

Most offenders against children remain in the community. They are not stopped. They are not treated. It is as much a social problem as is drug abuse and, like drugs, it is not best resolved by recourse to the criminal law.

CHILDREN AND CRIME

Children are our future. It makes sense to invest some of our time and resources in them; not only for the benefits that it will bring to them in the long term, but for the benefits it will bring to us by having the next generation developed to its full and proper potential.

As with all investments, in this case too there will be some gains and some losses — the value of some of those in whom we invest will increase more than the value of others. The value of some will fall, despite all that we invest in them. The market will move up in some stocks and down in others, and up and down, over time, in individual cases. We can all enjoy the gains; but we have to find ways of dealing with the losses, too. Sometimes the losses, reflected in criminal activity, are going to have to be dealt with by society as a whole.

I have made the economic comparison for a reason. A financial investor learns to cut his or her losses by identifying why they occurred and avoiding behaviours that are likely to see them continue or be repeated. He or she learns from experience — that of him/herself and of others — and applies those lessons. However, the community, confronted by criminal behaviour in children (and in adults, for that matter) doesn't ask 'why' or institute programs to prevent repetition; it reacts by condemning the person in whom its collective investment has failed. That is as useful as striking off a company because its share price went down after you bought in. You are still the loser, with no hope of recouping the loss. As part of the investment in our future we must find appropriate ways of dealing effectively with children who commit crimes. Those children will not go away. They will still be with us when they turn 18 and they will be acting then in ways that they are learning now unless we can change that learning. And as part of our investment in them we must deal more sympathetically and productively with those who are the victims of the crimes of those whose learning did not change as they reached adulthood.

It is a cycle. The abused of today become the abusers of tomorrow. In early 1999 a survey conducted at a NSW juvenile justice centre (Reiby) found that 87 per cent of inmates had been officially notified as abused children, 63 per cent on three or more occasions. Eighty-five per cent had alcohol or other drug problems and a significant number had mental health problems.

Unless we adults are able by our conduct to create conditions which will allow and encourage the young to accept society's laws and its processes, they will continue to flout them in the future. More children will grow to become abusers and the next generation of victims will be created. They, in turn, will rebel. And so on ...

Five: Starting at Home

*Women cause a lot of problems by nagging,
bitching and emotionally hurting men. Men
cannot bitch back, for hormonal reasons,
and often have no recourse but violence.*

UNIDENTIFIED NSW MAGISTRATE

In March 1999 New South Wales had a state election. As
is customary at such times, and despite vigorous denials by
both sides of politics, there was a law and order auction.
Once again the major parties intoned the election mantra of
more police, more powers, more prisons. We heard about
thousands of police to be plucked from the air, about zero
tolerance policing, about grid sentencing, about the naming
and shaming of juvenile offenders and there was much more
tough talk on addressing alleged terror in the streets. There
was not a word about domestic violence (for which a better
label would be violence against women, for that is what it
is). And remember, the Opposition leader at the time was
a woman.

In 1998 a Prevent Domestic Violence conference in
Adelaide had been barely mentioned in the media. When
South Australia launched a Silent Witness campaign it was
hardly noticed. (The silent witnesses in question are children

who witness violence to their mothers in their homes.)

By 2000 that was beginning to change. The Federal Government had commissioned a Young People and Domestic Violence survey and its findings were prominently reported. It found that attitudes to violence were affected by exposure to parental domestic violence and that an atmosphere of secrecy surrounded it. It also found, significantly, that more than a third of teenage girls experienced a violent dating relationship. One in seven had been sexually assaulted by a boyfriend.

A senior academic stated that the boys involved were merely expressing the values of society: '. . . one in four households suffers from domestic violence . . . we need to recognise this isn't happening in a vacuum.' Homegrown violence is reinforced by its portrayal as 'normal' in the entertainment media.

The myth concerning domestic violence is that it does not exist. Especially not in Australia! But it is a global issue from which we are not excepted and surveys show that as many as 40 per cent of Australian women in relationships with men experience domestic violence. Why is it not given the prominence it deserves? Is it really because the community does not think of it, as it does of other kinds of more public violence, as a law and order issue, a criminal justice issue? Is domestic violence regarded simply as some sort of 'secret women's business', or at least secret family business?

Domestic violence is usually secret. It happens in the home and what happens there is generally regarded as private. Domestic violence when it occurs is a feature of a private relationship between a man and a woman. That relationship may not be marriage or a settled 'partnership' of any kind. There is a significant number of young women who are in relationships with males who think they have to dominate girls to 'keep them in line' and to show themselves as 'real men'. Girlfriends are possessions; sex is a competitive sport between boys, not a part of a relationship with a girl. How often is there talk about 'scoring' with a female?

Many girls and women are influenced by learned social expectations — that they be patient, giving, trying to please and to comfort others. They should subject themselves to males. Many girls have low self-esteem or feel worthless without a boyfriend and are vulnerable as a result. They may accept almost any male and be dominated by him. Much more effort needs to be made to fortify and protect against violence younger females who are not living in relationships with males. 'Date rape' is seriously under-reported. Victims who do not recognise forced sex as unacceptable do not seek help.

In Britain in the eighteenth century there was a law that said a husband could beat his wife, but with a rod no thicker than his thumb, in order to maintain discipline. Provisions of this kind reflected deeply embedded attitudes that were imported into Australia in 1788. In the 1850s a sarcastic Sydney newspaper editorial observed: 'It seems to be one of the beauties of a free country that a man can beat his wife to his heart's content.' Attitudes of that kind survive to this day, and in many social contexts. They flourish in all cultures. They are manifested at all socio-economic levels. Some consider it still to be a man's right and responsibility to control 'his' woman's behaviour, and many set out to do so in a very crude fashion. Their mates often approve. A study commissioned by the Commonwealth Office of the Status of Women in 1995 found that one in five Australians believed that there are some circumstances in which it is acceptable for a husband to use physical force against his wife to impose his will.

There is still widespread ignorance of the dynamics of domestic violence, in particular of its cycles of tension, aggression and contrition growing more frequent — and more violent — with each repeat. The woman moves through phases of denial, self-blame, seeking help (in few cases), ambivalence and (in some cases) eventually living without violence.

The abuse may be physical or sexual (both of which constitute criminal offences), emotional or economic. The man's intention in each case is to control the woman.

Often the victim is blamed. She is asked: 'What did you do to make him hit you?' If the woman remains in the relationship (perhaps rationalising it by such responses as, 'At least he doesn't hit the children'), she is taken to accept it. If she leaves she is blamed for having failed to keep the family together.

Sometimes the woman dies. 'Intimate homicides' (the killing of a partner or former partner) comprise about a third of all homicides in Australia. (The highest proportion is in the Northern Territory and the lowest in Queensland. New South Wales is somewhere in the middle.) About four-fifths of these homicides are a male killing a female. About 40 women a year are killed in New South Wales as a result of domestic violence, half of them by guns and a quarter by knives. In the 1996 Australian *Heroines of Fortitude Report*, a Western Australian study found that Aboriginal women were 36 times more likely to be victims of spousal abuse than non-Aboriginal women.

Usually the woman is not killed, merely devastated: physically, emotionally, spiritually and financially. The stability of the family is threatened. There is an 80 per cent chance of children witnessing the violence. The effects on the children can be just as bad as if they had been attacked themselves: children learn that violence is an acceptable way to address problems or to control others. They learn not to trust any authority figure, even among their peers. They become socially awkward. Academic progress is interrupted. They become more prone to criminal behaviour and drug use, physical and psychological illness, behavioural problems and developmental delays. They become, in later life, less competent contributors to the common good, less valuable members of the workforce, customers of the courts, and their learned attitudes are perpetuated in turn by further violence.

In 1997, 39 960 complaints for personal violence protection orders (AVOs) were brought in the Local Court of New South Wales, about two-thirds of them for domestic protection. (AVO stands for 'apprehended violence order'. If a person complains to a court and satisfies it that on the balance of probabilities he or she has reasonable grounds to fear, and does fear, violence, harassment, molestation, intimidation or suchlike behaviour by another person, the court may make an order prohibiting certain conduct by that other person. The parties may, but need not, be in a domestic relationship.) In 1998 there were 49 611 complaints made.

In Victoria the figures were 10 891 in 1995–96 and 11 402 in 1996–97. Sometimes orders have to be made urgently. In New South Wales in 1997, 7555 telephone interim orders were made by the Local Court and 9660 in 1998.

Some Local Courts have 'family days' on which you can see the sad procession of anxious women, often pushing prams and strollers. They do not have the assistance of legal aid (which discriminates against women in that respect) and most must somehow fend for themselves. The domestic violence victims in the figures I have quoted are the ones who have sought outside help. It may be overstating the matter to say that they are the tip of the iceberg, but they are certainly only a part of the problem. Only about 20 per cent of women affected seek help outside the family.

Many myths in this area prevail. These include:

- That wife assault is caused by mental illness; it is said that a 'normal' male would not have done what is alleged to have happened. But no, the incidence of violence against women is too high, well above the incidence of relevant mental illness in the relevant male population. This is merely an attempt to excuse the male's behaviour as something that he could not help.
- That alcohol causes it; again, it is something the male could not prevent because he was drunk. But no, by reducing inhibitions alcohol simply makes it easier to act out impulses that are suppressed in the sober state.
- That the men are under stress; acting violently to a woman somehow relieves the normal pressures of life. But why not beat up a workmate, a neighbour, the postman? Why not any other male? Why is it OK to release frustration by beating up a woman, one who is close?
- That it is caused by poverty or low status; somehow a sense of inferiority or oppression justifies such antisocial conduct. But no, many 'successful' men beat their wives. Perpetrators are to be found in all walks of life and at all socioeconomic levels.
- That women provoke it; again, the violent conduct is sought to be justified on the basis that it is merely providing

women with their just deserts. But no, the violence is not proportionate to any conduct by women (in most cases), even if that could provide some measure of excuse. Usually the women are doing whatever they can to avoid the violence.

• That immigrant women tolerate it because of their culture; the argument of the ignorant bigot. No, immigrant women are trapped (like non-immigrant women who have nowhere else to go) by being in a strange environment, not knowing what avenues of assistance may be available, having no or little facility in the local language, and being without the support of family and friends.

There is a social cost to domestic violence. Financially, hundreds of millions of dollars each year are eaten up in medical expenses, counselling, lost productivity, dealing with the inter-generational violence that often follows, income support, emergency accommodation, police, courts and corrective services. Violence against women consumes more police time than any other call on police services, except traffic accidents. In 1998 the NSW Police Service responded to 76 733 incidents of domestic violence — an average of nearly one every seven minutes around the clock. A recent study in South Australia put the annual cost of domestic violence for that state alone at $100 million. The human costs are obvious.

Domestic violence is a crime. Society must seek to reduce and prevent it. When it occurs it must be dealt with as a crime.

Despite all that has been done by government and non-government agencies to prevent domestic violence and to assist after the event, in the 25 years since the problem was recognised and the fight against it began, the incidence of violence against women has not reduced. That will not occur, it seems, until we move further down the path to equality of the sexes in all contexts — different, yes, but equal. Male dominance and power, a legacy of our traditional patriarchal society, must give way for that to occur. It must be recognised that the abuse of women and children arises from their subordinate status in the social hierarchy. A change of that kind requires education, economic and social change, alongside reinforcement from the criminal justice system (which can itself, unfortunately, complicate the situation by, for example, separating the breadwinner from the family). When that is rectified — when the proper status of women and children is acknowledged universally — there will be condemnation of violence against them and society will order itself accordingly.

There have been specific initiatives relating to domestic violence on the international scene. On 12 December 1997 the UN adopted the Resolution on the Elimination of Violence Against Women. Annexed to the resolution were Model Strategies and Practical Measures on the Elimination of Violence Against Women in the Field of Crime Prevention and Criminal Justice, dealing with criminal law and procedure, police, sentencing and corrections, victim support and assistance, health and social services, training, research and evaluation, crime prevention measures, international cooperation and follow-up activities. Various conferences have been held to develop plans of action based upon these strategies.

A UN Special Rapporteur on Violence Against Women was appointed, and adopted the classification of violence against women: violence in the family, violence in the community and violence by the state. It must be recognised, however, that these categories may overlap — particular incidents may fall into more than one category.

The federal Minister for Justice released a report in the first half of 1999 entitled *Ending Domestic Violence? Programs for Perpetrators*. The report recommends a much stronger emphasis on responding to perpetrators of domestic violence through the criminal justice system, with mandatory attendance at programs utilised as an appropriate sentencing option. But resources (funds) are needed for such programs and they are not presently being provided. And such programs can deal only with perpetrators who have been exposed and then only the proportion of those who have come before the courts.

What is also needed is to persuade victims that it is right to come forward and report. They must first be helped to escape from the trap. Money will be needed. Women must be persuaded to ensure that their experiences, needs and concerns are understood. Nor should we lose sight of the fundamental problem of the inequality of the sexes.

Another important strategy, if we are to prevent tragic outcomes in these cases, is to renew attention on reducing the number of firearms in the community.

PREVENTION IS ALWAYS BETTER THAN CURE

Educational campaigns can succeed in conjunction with special police programs.

Think of drink-driving. Despite a bit of backsliding reported in the second half of 1999 in some places, there has been an enormous attitudinal change to drink-driving across the country, even among the boofheaded male population.

Think of child sexual abuse. Until comparatively recently it was hidden. Now it is not. Community attitudes and responses have changed. A climate of intolerance is developing: it is being recognised that there is a problem and that it needs to be dealt with. We know now that child sexual abuse has been with us for a long time and that we must combine our efforts to reduce it.

The relationship between child sexual abuse and domestic violence should not be forgotten. The offender's use of violence towards the child's mother may be used to impart clear messages of fear to the child and also to render the mother unavailable to the child, perhaps because of her pre-occupation with safety for herself and the emotional effect violence may have had on her. The child becomes available for abuse. However, even where domestic violence is used as a strategy by offenders to get their way in some other respect, most mothers do not know of the sexual abuse of their children and many respond protectively of the family unit when they find out about it. That response is slowly changing to more appropriate condemnation.

Child sexual abuse is relevant in other ways. The Women's Safety Survey, conducted Australia-wide in 1996, made many detailed findings about violence against women. It found that 'a history of violent victimization, whether as a child or an adult, predicts future victimization'. In other words, women who had experienced physical or sexual violence were more likely to experience it in the future. Perhaps they had learned to be victims, or at least, not to seek help to avoid victimisation.

The survey also showed that in this cycle of violence, persons who experience physical or sexual abuse as children have an increased risk as adults of abusing their own children.

People in the workplace are well placed to make a significant contribution to easing these problems. There are, no doubt, opportunities for businesses to become partners in programs already under way or contemplated by the Department for Women, the Attorney General's Department, the Victims of Crime Bureau, the Office of the DPP and many other agencies, state and federal, which do recognise the importance of this issue to us all.

There are barriers. Our present business culture focuses on survival and reform in a climate of competition for resources. Uncertainty about the future narrows that focus to the individual company or person. 'Mateship' survives. A downside of mateship is lack of consideration of the problems and inequalities of those who are not mates.

There is a resulting lack of attention to big issues, to the overall good (in both national and international contexts). That climate or culture assists in hiding from the workplace, and from business, problems created by domestic violence. But business can act to help change attitudes.

All persons in responsible positions should learn to recognise the signs of abuse of women, just as teachers are trained to recognise child abuse. Businesses can put in place appropriate reactive programs for support and counselling. They can also be proactive and publicise the evils, put up posters in staff rooms, dining rooms and waiting areas, target male workers with propaganda. The message can be carried into clubs, pubs, casinos and sporting venues. An attitude of openness can be fostered and emphasis put on the costs in both human and financial terms.

Similar strategies can be adopted by government agencies and in all institutions where women make contact with those outside their immediate families.

Radio commentators and tabloid journalists could also promote anti-violence instead of criticising women's advocates as 'feminazis'. The criminal law can respond in ways additional to those suggested by the Minister for Justice in her 1999 report. In December 1998 an international panel of experts met in Vancouver, Canada, to develop an International Criminal Justice Strategy to Eliminate Violence Against Women. Among the initiatives discussed were the inclusion of a provision condemning violence against women in the constitutions of nation states; the criminalisation of sexual harassment in the workplace; the criminalising of those who purchase certain sexual services; the broadening of conduct to be included in sexual assault or rape provisions; recognising as inoperative consent obtained by threat; imposing the onus of proof of consent onto the accused; prohibitions on stalking; further support for complainants in court proceedings; specialised family violence courts; and the improvement of police training and practice in the investigation of allegations of abuse. Some of this has been done or is under way in Australia, but more needs to be done to translate the right messages into the community generally.

Women are the majority of our population. Their children are our future. Men will stop abusing them only when they recognise that the climate has changed and that such conduct has been frozen out.

Six: Stopping

Some of the causes of increases and decreases in particular crimes are unavoidable. Some influences will produce results regardless of what we do or say. There are demographic features — consequences of the makeup and distribution of the population. Some crime is correlated with particular ages. Most offenders are males in the 15 to 25 age range so the post-war babyboomers, and now their offspring, have produced bubbles of crime simply by growing up. More people of a certain age, more crime of an expected type. Some crime is correlated with ethnic origin. Some is committed more by one sex.

There is the influence of drug markets. As I have noted, there will always be drugs; but there are fashions in drug type, there are changes in the way the markets operate and there are changes in the participants. Sometimes violence is associated with drug markets, sometimes not. The nature and extent of those markets will influence the level and incidence of property crime.

The level of economic prosperity in the community also has an influence. People make choices to support themselves by legal or illegal occupations. If there are plenty of opportunities for legitimate work, criminals may make a cost/benefit assessment and choose that over continuing a life of crime. This may be a consideration influenced by age. A would-be young drug pusher or car thief may choose instead to work in a shop, but if the job disappears in an economic downturn or the now-older person gets bored and has no skills for advancement, he or she may revert to a life of crime, but crime of the type committed by his or her now-older age group.

The total number of intimate partner homicides has in fact declined over time. The reason for that may be clear enough: social changes have reduced the number of long-term intimate partners.

The level of imprisonment in a society influences the crime rate. For some types of crime (for example, drug dealing) an imprisoned offender is quickly replaced by another. However, the incarceration of large numbers of violent males until they mellow certainly reduces the amount of violent offending in the community. It is an expensive option, however. In New South Wales it costs about $65 000 per annum to keep a prisoner in maximum security (about $47 000 per annum in minimum security), and prisons are not crime-free themselves. They also provide an excellent environment for the learning of new criminal skills.

We can learn from the United States in this as in other matters — learn from, not follow! There the crime rate increased from World War II until about 1970. It has been falling since. In the decade of the 1970s the prison population in the United States doubled from 250 000 to 500 000. It cost

US$9 billion per annum extra to do that, alongside a 15 per cent drop in crime. The next doubling, from 500 000 to 1 million added another US$18 billion per annum to the bill — twice as much — but with only another 15 per cent reduction in crime.

In late 1999 the Justice Policy Institute of Washington DC reported that on 1 January 1900 there were 57 070 prisoners in the United States — 122 per 100 000 head of population. It calculated that on 1 January 2000 there would be 1 982 084 — 725 per 100 000. That costs about US$40 billion, more than the public expenditure on colleges and universities.

There are more men in the United States under correctional control than are registered as unemployed, which, added to the 3.5 million on probation or parole, means that one in 37 US citizens is under corrective supervision (enough for a city of 5.5 million, which would be the second largest in the United States!). The Institute estimated that there would be two million inmates by 15 February 2000 and 2 073 969 by the end of the year. (Prisoners are not able to vote in the United States, so many citizens are disenfranchised.)

It is estimated the doubling of the prison population to two million, will cost about US$55 billion per annum extra: but for what benefit? Even if it does have some small influence on the crime rate, just how cost effective is incarceration as a means of crime control? And is it any different in Australia?

The Australian Institute of Criminology has been keeping track. In the period 1982 to 1998 there was an average annual increase in the imprisonment of people of imprisonable age of 4.2 per cent. There were 9826 prisoners in 1982 and 19 906 in 1998. In June 1999 there were 20 504 (over one-third — 7240 — being in New South Wales). The simplistic talkback 'entertainers' might say that this is because the crime rate has been increasing, but they would be wrong (again).

In *Sentencing Reform and Penal Change* (1999) Arie Freiberg and Stuart Ross examined the relationship between crime rates and imprisonment rates in Australia in relation to the offences of murder, assault, break, enter and steal, and theft. They demonstrated that rather than being a direct consequence of crime rates, imprisonment rates may be a result of sentencing practices, the length of time offenders are required to remain in prison and the proportion of offenders sentenced to prison.

Just as crime rates are not much help in many cases in predicting imprisonment rates, so numbers of prisoners are not much help in measuring crime rates.

Between 1992 and 1997 the rate of violent crime in New York State fell by 38.6 per cent and the murder rate by 54.5 per cent while the prison population grew by 30 per week. In California in the same period the violent crime rate fell by only 23 per cent and the murder rate by 28 per cent while the prison population grew by 270 per week.

By way of further illustration: between 1987 and 1995 the imprisonment rate in the United States overall increased by 124 per cent, but the crime rate increased by only 2 per cent; in the same period in the Netherlands the imprisonment rate increased by 100 per cent (i.e. doubled), but the crime rate increased by 8 per cent. What do these figures mean? In short, locking up more people does not reduce crime across the board, especially serious violent crime.

Some forces *can* have an effect in reducing crime. There are some policy initiatives, institutional forces and community efforts that can have a positive effect. It is those that we should give more attention to in the future — the logic — instead of the perpetuation of unproductive myths about crime and 'getting tough' about locking away our social failures.

POSSIBLE NEW DIRECTIONS

Far more has been accomplished for the welfare and progress of mankind by preventing bad actions than doing good ones.

WILLIAM LYON MACKENZIE KINJ

If poverty is the mother of crime, stupidity is its father.

WILLIAM LYON MACKENZIE KINJ

Research carried out over the last 200 years, since at least the time of Jeremy Bentham, confirms that informal social control is more effective in preventing crime than formal controls, such as police and prisons.

We all live in institutions (social structures in the community) we depend on them and society would not survive without them. They are familial, educational, social, economic and political in nature. In their own ways they reduce individual motivation to commit crime, they supply effective controls to curb such behaviour and they protect their members against the criminal behaviour of others.

Families teach us the difference between appropriate and inappropriate behaviour and reinforce or punish accordingly. Educational institutions also reinforce moral values and broaden our vision. They and other institutions impose informal and formal social controls upon us. Economic institutions, such as our employment environment, satisfy our basic needs, help us adapt to the broader environment and rank us according to responsibilities and rewards. Political institutions apply resources for collective goals.

Most of us have complex connections to a number of institutions that either deter us from criminal conduct or make it difficult to get away with. Those connections teach us *obedience to the unenforceable* — obedience to standards and expectations that cannot be enforced except by the individual's choice, but upon which society nevertheless depends. If that fails, the final hurdle — and reckoning — is provided by the state institutions, such as the police and courts.

Therefore, individuals who are well institutionalised (socialised or morally responsible) are self-regulators. There is an argument that if social institutions lose their ability to regulate their members, individuals will act as they please, selfishly, without effective control and with no regard for those affected. Institution-building is therefore one effective way to improve crime prevention. Relationships need to be strengthened. We have stakeholders in all our actions and they need to be considered in all that we do. Community needs to be strengthened.

Economically disadvantaged people are more likely to commit a wide range of offences. Many people cannot accept going without things, even rich people, but they are in a minority and are motivated simply by greed. Poor people may take what they believe should be theirs; but they also miss out in so many direct and indirect ways on what society should be providing, and that can lead to crimes of frustration and despair. People become resentful. Resentment can become anger and anger can lead to crime. The economic health of a community where crime is prevalent requires attention.

Problems are presently brewing in this regard in New South Wales and around the country. Poor, welfare-dependent families are moving out of Sydney in search of cheaper living. In 1998 across Australia 44 per cent of children under 15 were living in low-income families that were entitled to greater than the minimum family welfare payments; that is, poor families. In country areas the number was up to 68 per cent. Up to a third of families were single-parent with up to 56 per cent of all families being on welfare. In one country NSW branch of the Department of Community Services, the workload has doubled every 18 months for the six years to 1999, including notifications for domestic violence, child abuse or neglect, drug, social and family problems. In 1999 it was able to deal with only 40 per cent of these notifications. Children leave school early, they leave home, they are unemployed, they abuse drugs, they steal. They lose social support and it is not replaced by government services. Without support they can become criminals.

Physical and psychological health are also important. Not surprisingly, there is a general correlation between decreased alcohol consumption and reduced crime. Policies directed towards controlling the availability of alcohol and the circumstances and level of its consumption will reduce crime. Many of us like a drink; but we should be encouraged by official policies to enjoy it in pleasant and convivial circumstances and not to use it as a means of getting drunk and releasing natural inhibitions and behaving in ways that society will later regret (not to mention the drinker . . .).

Reducing the consumption of illicit drugs will also have an impact on crime in ways that I have already noted.

Ordinary people can make some difference to the crime rate. Organised neighbourhood activities can contribute.

Community meetings and practical initiatives to address specific local problems should be encouraged. And these are cheap. Individually, ordinary people can be assisted to decide to cut down on alcohol and drug consumption, to make the choice to work, to take pride in their community and protect it.

Educated people in good health, living in comfortable homes, with stable relationships (of whatever makeup), with strong social ties and steady jobs and enjoyable leisure pursuits usually do not commit crimes. Even politicians know that.

We should be focusing on maximising some or all of those opportunities and strengthening the associations that prevent crime in the first place, not perpetuating myths about the effectiveness of more police, zero tolerance policing, more and heavier sentences, more prisons and 'wars' on particular types of offending. That path is well-trodden, quick, cheap (in the short term only) and easy; it just involves a bit of noise and can be taken before the next election — but the path extends forever. The truly effective route is more difficult and, goodness me, it might not produce measurable results until after the next election!

Crime will be with us forever and we have a budding crop of criminals right now. In New South Wales alone, as I have noted earlier, there are about 20 000 notifications for child abuse and neglect each year. At least a quarter of those children will end up involved in crime. New criminals are therefore coming on line at about one every two hours.

Families need support in the early days of child rearing. For those in difficulty there should be frequent home visits by nurses and other professionals while there is an infant in the home — the Commission for Children and Young People has recognised the value of such visits. There should be weekly home visits by pre-school teachers at the next stage. For delinquent and at-risk children and adolescents there should be family therapy and parent training available. Schools should have specially developed programs for innovation, communication, reinforcement of clear and consistent norms, the teaching of social competency skills and the coaching of high-risk youth in thinking skills.

These programs, which start at the beginning and not at the end where we 'undertakers' operate, have been tested in other communities and found to be effective. The empirical data are available. They are useful tools in the armoury of weapons available to us to reduce crime and improve our society, if only we could tap the political will to open the armoury door. Our challenge as citizens is to do just that.

Seven: What Right to Silence?

I know it's cannabis oil and it's a prohibited import. I put it there myself. But I know my rights and that's all I'm saying.

ARRIVING INTERNATIONAL TRAVELLER TO
CUSTOMS OFFICER

(Enough said!)

There is no right to silence. Sorry ... that's another popular myth.

In our system of criminal justice we have a collection of notions which together are often described as 'the right to silence'. But they are a grab-bag of immunities, or protections, that accompany a suspect or defendant or accused on the journey through the gateways of the process of criminal justice. They are various and have been created and qualified over time by legislation and court decisions. Let us consider them.

A suspect is under no obligation to say anything to investigating police. A defendant or accused in a court hearing is under no obligation even to participate, beyond just being there. (And even if he or she refuses to turn up or is removed because of misconduct, the hearing may still proceed.) Generally speaking there can be no penalty for refusing to take part in the process, no adverse inference (or unfavourable conclusion) can be drawn and no adverse comment can be made about the person's silence or lack of cooperation.

Many people say that some of this is contrary to common sense and operates to the detriment of society, that in this day and age, when just about everybody has had at least a basic education and (at least if adult and sane) knows right from wrong, a court or jury should be able to draw whatever inferences it thinks proper from the behaviour, in court or outside, of someone accused of a crime. They say that discretions could be built into procedures to safeguard the truly disadvantaged against real injustice but still allow people to be judged by their conduct. (Some go further and say that if a person, having enjoyed all the protections of the criminal justice system, has still been hauled before the court, then he or she should really show why there should not be a conviction.)

Those who claim to speak for suspects and accused persons, however, maintain that such immunities are necessary to protect the innocent against abuse of power by the state and to ensure that the guilty are not dealt with unfairly. Is that a myth?

As in many arguments about the criminal law, it is necessary to strike a balance.

IMMUNITIES

In simple terms the immunities or protections recognised by the law (and included in the general description 'right to silence') include the following:

- Nobody can be compelled, on pain of punishment, to answer questions put by somebody else.
- Nobody can be compelled to provide answers to questions that may incriminate them.
- Criminal suspects cannot be compelled to answer questions put by police or other investigators.
- Once persons have been charged with criminal offences they cannot be questioned by police or other investigators about the subject matter of the charges (unless they agree).
- Defendants and accused persons in criminal hearings cannot be compelled to answer questions or give evidence.
- Generally, persons on trial cannot have adverse comments made about them or adverse inferences drawn against them because of failure to answer questions before trial or to give evidence during it. (There is a limited, technical exception.)

Argument about these protections usually relates to questioning by police; pre-trial disclosure by the prosecution; pre-trial disclosure by the defence; and silence during the trial.

QUESTIONING BY POLICE

As I have noted earlier, a confession that is extracted by mistreatment of a suspect is likely to be unreliable. It is likely to have been made, whether true or not, just to stop the mistreatment. In such circumstances it may well not be the truth. This was recognised by judges in past centuries and so rules developed that whenever a police officer had decided to charge a suspect or had sufficient grounds for doing so, the suspect had to be warned or 'cautioned' that he or she was entitled to remain silent. The form of the caution varies from place to place. The caution in Australia is different from what you hear in 'The Bill' because UK law is now different from Australian law.

There are some very limited exceptions to this rule; for example, a driver of a motor vehicle that is pulled over can be required to provide name and address and a driving licence; some limited information must also be provided by juveniles who attract the attention of police in certain circumstances.

The caution rule has been extended to give the courts discretion to refuse to admit into evidence any answers to questions by persons in authority that have been obtained by unlawful or unfair methods (and extended further to other evidence obtained by such means).

These rules and procedures are no longer very controversial. They are seen as necessary to deter improper conduct by those in positions of power, like police officers. Inquiries such as the Royal Commission into the NSW Police Service have shown very clearly that if there are not strong controls in place over bodies like police forces, there will be improper conduct and corruption. Unprofessional police will always be quick to exploit any loophole in procedures to achieve what they regard as the 'right' result. That may extend to pressuring a suspect or fabricating evidence if they think they can get away with it. That is why the courts must have rules in place that will frustrate improper short cuts and the abuse of private rights. Sometimes, however, the rules may appear to frustrate the achieving of justice. A balance must be struck, once again, and that must be done in practice, in the circumstances of the individual case.

The rules in Australia about receiving admissions into evidence have been strengthened to the benefit of all parties (including the police, who no longer have unjustified allegations of improper behaviour made against them in court) by the video-recording of interrogations in police stations and by rules that have been made about excluding from evidence answers and statements that have not been videotaped.

Pre-trial Disclosure by the Prosecution

When a person has been charged with a criminal offence and the matter is to go to court, a full brief of the relevant evidence available must be provided to the defendant in advance of the hearing. He or she knows, from documents and other things provided, what allegation is made and what evidence is available to prove it.

If there is a summary hearing in the Local Court, the defendant has the opportunity there (as described earlier) to test that evidence and to provide any available evidence in defence, if that is desired. At a committal hearing in a serious case in the Local Court, the defendant has a limited opportunity to test some witnesses (if there are special or substantial reasons why cross-examination should be allowed) and can also lead evidence in defence before the magistrate decides whether or not to commit for trial. If there is to be a trial, any additional evidence that the prosecution seeks to rely upon must be provided to the accused in advance of the trial. The prosecution makes full disclosure of its case before trial. That is a duty. It is a practice of all Australian Directors of Public Prosecutions.

Defence Non-disclosure

By contrast, a defendant or accused is under no obligation to disclose anything in advance of the hearing to the prosecution or to the court and often does not do so.

In New South Wales the only exceptions to that statement are where an accused for trial relies on alibi evidence and the witnesses who will say that he or she was elsewhere at the time of the offence must be disclosed; where a person accused of murder seeks to rely on the defence of substantial impairment by abnormality of mind and evidence in support must be disclosed; and where tendency, coincidence or hearsay evidence is to be led then notice must be given.

Generally speaking, however, the defence (by which I mean collectively the defendant or the accused, his or her representative and witnesses, and evidence in support of the defence 'case') may remain silent until the hearing. There is no requirement on a defendant or accused to do anything more than plead not guilty — and even if the person refuses to do that, a not guilty plea will be entered in consequence.

That means that the prosecution is in the dark about what issues are to be contested. What is the trial going to be about? In a rape case, for example, is the accused going to deny intercourse or to say that it happened, but with consent? (Some men have tried to have it both ways!) In a case of dishonesty, is the accused going to deny taking the money or to say that it was taken under a claim of right; that is, it was lawfully his or hers to take?

This can have serious implications for the running of trials. The prosecution is expected to have all its evidence and all its witnesses present, and be ready to prove strictly, in accordance with all the legal rules, every element or ingredient of the offence that has been charged. A great deal of work and the involvement of many people is required to get a case to that stage, at the cost of labour, time, money, inconvenience and anguish to a great many people, in both the private and public sectors.

Instead of allowing accused persons to thumb their noses at the courts, in effect, and say 'you prove it', where is the unfairness or injustice in requiring them to tell the prosecution in advance what the trial is going to be about — what defence is going to be run, what issues are going to be raised, what witnesses might be excused because there is not going to be a challenge to their evidence?

The idiocy of the present arrangements can be seen when one considers the evidence of expert witnesses. Experts may be drawn from many special fields to consider the evidence and express opinions in the course of trials about what happened, why things happened or what will happen in the future. To take one example: if a person is on trial for murder, he or she may wish to call psychiatrists to give evidence about his or her mental state at the time (this not being 'substantial impairment', a special defence where notice is required of expert evidence in order for it to be relied upon). That evidence might be disclosed for the first time when the witness gives evidence in the trial. There is no opportunity for the prosecution to test the evidence. There is also no opportunity to have the accused examined by another expert; that can only be done by consent of the accused. The prosecution then has to whistle up a psychiatrist to sit in the back of the court, listen to the evidence being given, make notes and then give evidence in reply as best he or she can.

To take another example: a person accused of dangerous driving causing death may wish to rely on the evidence of an expert that a mechanical fault in the vehicle caused the accident, not his or her manner of driving. That evidence need not be disclosed until the expert is in the witness box. The vehicle involved by then may have been junked.

In both these cases, not only is the task made unfair and unjust for the prosecutor (who represents the community), but the accused loses the opportunity of persuading the prosecution, by the production in advance of the expert evidence, of having the proceedings discontinued before further time, effort, expense and agony are incurred by all concerned, or at least of having the proceedings shortened so that the real issues are dealt with expeditiously and with the smallest necessary costs to all concerned.

Defence ambushes of these kinds result from the so-called 'right to silence'. Defence representatives protest that if they are required to tell the prosecution what the argument is, then the prosecution will prepare its case to defeat the argument. There are at least two responses to that: first, the prosecution can only have recourse to what is legitimately available in support of its case (it cannot make evidence out of nothing) and secondly, isn't the whole process supposed to be directed at discovering the truth? A third response might come from the Duc de la Rochefoucald: 'Silence is the best tactic for him who distrusts himself.'

Silence at Trial

It is possible for an accused person to remain silent and do nothing throughout a criminal trial. That rarely happens, but when it does the prosecution must go through all the proper procedures to prove its case. Nor can the court generally conclude against the interests of the accused for that reason.

If an accused person does not give evidence in the trial, the prosecution (in New South Wales) cannot comment on that to the jury, directly or indirectly. A co-accused can, and so can the judge (but in a very limited fashion in particular circumstances). This situation also differs from one state to another. Juries, of course, are not stupid, but in law they are not permitted to draw any adverse inference from an accused's silence beyond any that may be directed by the judge (and that rarely happens). One can only speculate how often juries flout the law.

REVIEW

There is a strong argument, I think, that the further along the criminal justice track a person goes — the more gateways he or she passes through — the more right the community has to expect him or her to cooperate with the process in a reasonable way. Criminal justice is expensive — we cannot afford to waste scarce resources that might be better spent on hospitals and schools and crime prevention in the first place.

When a person is first confronted by police there may be every good reason why that person should be legally protected to the greatest extent practicable. At that stage, usually, there is only a suspicion of guilt in the mind of a police officer. But once the evidence against the person has been examined by a magistrate and an order made that there should be a trial, an independent judicial mind will have been brought to bear on the matter and there will have been some assessment of the likelihood of guilt. It is time for the accused to stop stonewalling. If he or she is innocent (wholly or partially, having at least a partial defence to the charge) then surely it is time for him or her to start showing how?

That person has had a duty, as a member of society, not to break the law. While that duty has been observed, he or she has had the protection of the right to silence (so-called) as it applies to all citizens not charged with an offence. The person should know that if that duty is not observed, then he or she will be dealt with fairly, but increasingly firmly as liability for the breach is progressively established.

Accused persons do not disclose anything by choice because time is on their side. They know that for as long as they continue to stonewall there is a hope — perhaps a faint one these days — that the wheels might yet fall off the prosecution case and that they might just scrape out of it. Perhaps a witness will disappear or die or some evidence might be lost, if they can only obstruct for long enough. There is a saying 'Justice delayed is justice denied' and so it can be in such circumstances, but for the community.

If the present arrangements are not to change, we need to ensure that our system works efficiently, that there are not lengthy delays for trials, that there are enough magistrates and judges to keep the wheels turning at an acceptable rate. Then we might eventually see a greater degree of cooperation from the defence side of the contest. (But there is every sign that such a day is a long time off.)

The right to silence, as practised in our system, is exploited by the guilty. Why would an innocent person not take every opportunity to protest that innocence from the earliest stage? What would you do if you were wrongly accused? And what would you do if you were rightly accused?

Criminal lawyers will say that I have over-simplified these issues, perhaps even trivialised them. I confess to the former.

There are many complex arguments about this issue being debated in many forums around Australia at present. Legislation is being contemplated to impose a measure of defence disclosure in contravention of the hallowed but misdescribed right to silence. But I believe that the issues can be summarised simply and that is what I have sought to do.

The NSW Government announced that in 2000 it would legislate to provide for pre-trial disclosure by the prosecution and to force, for the first time in Australia, more general disclosure by the defence in some circumstances. Stand by . . .

Eight: Sentencing

Criminals are getting off all the time.
Sentences are not tough enough.

CHORUS

Let us go back a bit, in fact, back to the start . . .

By definition, crime is offensive. It is conduct carried out against rules that we have made for our own wellbeing. Some crime is more offensive than other crime. A speeding driver commits a criminal offence, is fined and loses points from his or her licence, but is not otherwise usually made the subject of public condemnation. But if while speeding the driver runs down and kills a child on a pedestrian crossing, there are some who are so offended that they would say that anything short of death — an eye for an eye — or at least an extremely lengthy gaol term, is too lenient a penalty.

Crime offends against our sense of social order and is personally offensive especially to those who become its victims. It can also be personally offensive to those who subsequently have to deal with its consequences, the 'undertakers' to whom I refer elsewhere.

Those consequences cannot be undone. It is never possible to restore all those affected by crime to the position that existed before. In the words of Omar Khayyam: 'The moving finger writes, and having writ, moves on; nor all thy piety nor wit shall lure it back to cancel half a line, nor all thy tears wash out a word of it.'

The criminal process cannot restore rights to those who have been deprived of them. There is much discussion these days about the means of achieving justice in particular situations, it being accepted that the criminal trial process is not the only means. What is justice? Does it mean people getting what they deserve? Who decides what is deserved, and what are the criteria? People talk of justice as the affirmation of human dignity and of deterrent justice, compensatory justice, rehabilitative justice and justice as exoneration. 'Restorative justice' is another catchphrase. These are issues for another time.

In earlier and more primitive times people gave in to their grief and rage. They exacted swift and summary punishment upon those caught doing them wrong. In some societies (such as parts of southern Italy) such action spawned vendettas, while in others (such as the highlands of Papua New Guinea) it developed into payback feuds, where tit-for-tat punishments continued through the generations, the origins lost in the mists of time and forgotten. There are remnants of these instincts in most human souls; the first reaction of most wronged individuals is an understandable lust for revenge. But as Francis Bacon so long ago pointed out, 'Revenge is a kind of wild justice; which the more man's nature runs to, the more ought law to weed it out'. In our form of society some centuries ago the responsibility for redressing criminal wrongs was taken from individuals by the state — the sovereign. The convenient fiction was developed that breaking the law breached the sovereign's peace and was therefore punishable by the agencies established for that purpose by the sovereign — eventually the police, the courts and the penal system. Part of the very justification for such a system is that it prevents people taking the law into their own hands: it prevents vigilantism and unregulated retribution.

When the role of punishment was 'nationalised' it became necessary to be clear about what the public institutions should do and why: on what basis, on what principles, with what justification, to what purpose should they act? More rules were needed.

For a time our public-response system adopted all the sorts of punishments that victims of crime might have liked to impose themselves, given the chance: death, flogging, outlawry, transportation, confiscation of all property, imprisonment, fine. No doubt there are individuals who would still like to see these things done to those who wrong them, who might thrill to the words of the English Chief Justice in 1660 as he sentenced those responsible for the death of King Charles I in 1649:

> The judgement of this court is that you be led back to the place from whence you came, and from thence to be drawn upon a hurdle to the place of execution, and there you shall be hanged by the neck and being alive shall be cut down, and your privy parts to be cut off, your entrails to be taken out of your body, and, you living, the same to be burned before your eyes, and your head to be cut off, your body to be divided into four quarters to be disposed of at the pleasure of the King, and the Lord have mercy on your soul.

(Some person actually did this to them! It is not known how the Lord reacted . . .)

Collectively we have moved beyond the primitive and learnt that it is ultimately in our interests to control and redirect those base urges. Our institutions have accepted, in the light of experience and guided by fundamental considerations of human rights and various religious and other social ethics, that there is a greater long-term benefit for all by approaching the problem in a more detached and formalised way.

If we are going to punish people we need to know why we are doing it and what we are achieving. These days the purposes of punishment are said by our highest courts and by the parliaments that prescribe the penalties they apply to be *deterrence*, *retribution* and *reform*. There is also an element of the *protection* of society from people who cannot safely live among us.

Deterrence assumes that we will all consider what may happen to us if we are caught doing wrong and will weigh this up before committing a crime. It operates *individually*, by showing the offender that if he or she offends in that way, he or she will be deprived of the liberty to live as he or she chooses. It operates *generally* by showing all other members of the community what will (possibly) happen to them if they act in the same way (but, importantly, only if they are caught!). Does it work? Let's look at a specific example taken from the *1998–99 NSW Police Service Annual Report*. In 1997 concern over an increase in the number of assaults against police prompted the government to increase the maximum penalties prescribed for such offences. Did the number of assaults go down? No, it went up by almost 10 per cent.

Retribution is a form of payback by society. It is a hangover from revenge, but this time it is the community generally, through its criminal justice agencies, that is demonstrating its disapproval of the offender's conduct by imposing a penalty. It is collective revenge and it does have a place in sentencing. It makes the community feel better.

Reform (or rehabilitation) of the offender is based on the notion that it is possible, given the right conditions, to convert criminals into law-abiding citizens by compulsion. It is a worthy objective and one that should be pursued, even if a lower priority must be given to it and the results are not often very encouraging. But reform is not going to be an option if the sentence imposed leaves the prisoner in despair, with no hope, no light at the end of the tunnel of the term of imprisonment. There has to be room left in the prisoner's future life for the reform to be demonstrated in practice, and for there to be some incentive for it in the first place. Contrition must come from within, but we should encourage it to emerge.

We have abolished the death penalty and the other more barbaric forms of revenge, such as flogging (although that persists in some other countries). We do not cut off hands for theft or stone people for adultery. We now rely upon imprisonment, pecuniary or financial penalties (fines, court and investigation costs orders, and confiscation orders taking from offenders their ill-gotten gains), conditional orders of various kinds (e.g. bonds and recognisances or release on conditions, suspended sentences) and some diversionary schemes that transfer the care of offenders from the courts to the community (e.g. diversionary conferencing, which brings criminals and victims face to face, and treatment programs for certain sex offenders and drug-addicted offenders).

The upper levels of punishment able to be imposed for particular offences, and the alternatives available, are set by the Parliament. In this way the collective will of the people, moderated by the need to act always in the general public interest and with regard to generally accepted standards of regulation, is reflected in both the maximum penalties prescribed and the latitude to be given to the courts. The courts — the third arm of government — must act within those legislated boundaries.

It is sometimes asserted by talkback 'entertainers' and

newspaper columnists (and those seeking their support) that the law and the courts are out of touch with what the community wants as the appropriate penalties for particular offences. Such comments usually follow publicity given to a penalty perceived as too lenient. Unfortunately, such publicity usually occurs over wholly exceptional cases, where either there are extraordinary circumstances applying or the judge has got it wrong (and judges are only human so that does sometimes happen). In the latter case a Crown appeal may be able to remedy the situation. In any case, one wonders just what is the community expectation (as distinct from the commentator's) and how this is known. Judges generally bear the brunt of the uninformed attacks that are launched on these occasions and for the reasons already explained (see Chapter 1 The Criminal Law in Action) they are not in a position to respond.

The punishment available in any case is fixed by Parliament, not the courts. If there is true community concern about the prescribed penalties then the community should have its representatives alleviate this by amending the relevant legislation. Further, it is simply not possible for anyone who has not witnessed the entire proceedings in court to have an understanding of all the considerations taken into account by the sentencing judge. How many talkback hosts have the means and take the time to weigh up all the circumstances considered by the judge? Do they even want to? How many newspaper columnists — or politicians — have the time and inclination to dig out the details assessed by the judge? A partial story better suits all their immediate purposes: the pursuit of ratings, circulation figures and public attention. Judges are a good whipping post because they cannot whip back. They have already laid their cards on the table by conducting the proceedings in open court and publicly providing comprehensive reasons for the penalty imposed. Their reasoning is transparent and public, if only the commentators would take the time and trouble to listen, read and report it responsibly and fully.

So are guilty people being set free? What has been happening with penalties in recent times?

CONVICTIONS AND SENTENCES

In November 1998 the NSW Bureau of Crime Statistics and Research reported on conviction rates (after both trial and plea of guilty) for a range of major offences in all courts for 1996. (Statistical studies often take time to complete and so are rarely up to the minute.) 'Conviction rates' means the proportion of convictions obtained (by plea of guilty or after trial) in all cases in specific categories of criminal offences coming before the courts. The Bureau found the conviction rates to have been (in round figures) as follows.

Criminal offence	Higher courts	Local courts
assault	80%	75%
sexual assault	60%	55%
child sexual assault	65%	40%
manslaughter	80%	
murder*	55%	
break and enter	90%	85%
robbery	90%	
fraud	90%	85%
dealing and trafficking in opiates	90%	90%

* The Bureau noted that many people who are acquitted of murder are convicted of manslaughter with consequential effect on the figures for those crimes.

It would seem that the courts are not in the business of wholesale release of those coming before them on serious criminal charges. The Bureau also presented some basic facts about sentencing for a range of offences in the Local, District and Supreme Courts over the period 1990 to 1997. It took into account the effect that the severity of the offence and previous convictions had on the penalty imposed. The Bureau referred to some of the current media hype about sentences and said:

> Part of the reason for the concern about leniency is a lack of public understanding about the sentencing process and how it can produce what seem to be large disparities in the outcomes and penalties for apparently similar crimes. This lack of under-standing can easily be manipulated by the media to create the impression that the courts are very haphazard in the way they deal with offenders.

This part of the report reaffirms the view that uninformed and hysterical outcries by media personalities, seizing on unusual or occasionally wrong decisions by the courts, make us think that all court decisions are wrong, or at least inconsistent and not what we should expect.

The survey of sentencing of those dealt with for the offences listed above (excepting manslaughter, murder and robbery) over the period 1990 to 1997 revealed that:

- the percentage imprisoned has remained stable or increased for each of the selected offences (in direct contradiction of claims that the courts have been setting criminals free); and
- the average prison sentence length imposed for each of the selected offences has generally remained stable (contradicting claims that sentences are getting shorter).

The Bureau concluded:

> This bulletin has shown that, despite the largely media-driven perception of court leniency, the NSW court system is not generally acquitting people and penalties have, if anything, become heavier since 1990. The courts also deal more harshly with offenders who commit more serious crimes and who have more serious criminal records.

In a later report in December 1999 the Bureau revealed that the number of women in prison in New South Wales has increased significantly in recent years (up 25 per cent in the previous year and 40 per cent in the previous five years), due to a higher number of convictions of women in the courts, a higher proportion of women being dealt with for offences that carry prison sentences and because 'courts are more readily handing down sentences of imprisonment'. It found sentence lengths for women have also increased.

Despite the ready availability of such facts, and their persuasiveness, politicians (especially) persist in proposing so-called 'get tough' reforms for the criminal justice system. Within three months of the release of the Bureau's 1998 findings, in the context of a state election campaign, the old unnecessary law and order auction was on again.

MANDATORY SENTENCES

Mandatory sentences, or mandatory minimum sentences, usually get a run at election times. Mandatory sentences are sentences that are prescribed by Parliament in such a way that the courts have no ability to decide an appropriate penalty in an individual case — the punishment has been set by Parliament to be imposed automatically and without alteration by the courts in all cases of that particular offence. Mandatory sentencing would be better described as mandatory imprisonment.

There is no doubt that Parliaments do have the power to prescribe such penalties and if they do so validly the courts must impose them. That is one outcome of our doctrine of the separation of powers, in this case between the legislature and the judiciary. Such laws are operating in the Northern Territory and Western Australia (for property offences, including those committed by juveniles) and also in New South Wales (see later in this chapter) and Queensland (where the only penalty for murder is life imprisonment). However, there are philosophical and practical objections to mandatory penalties (for anything other than minor regulatory offences, e.g. traffic offences), which deprive the sentencing court of any discretion in the punishment that it might impose. Former Chief Justice of Australia, Sir Garfield Barwick, said in a judgment:

> Ordinarily the court with the duty of imposing punishment has a discretion as to the extent of the punishment to be imposed; and sometimes a discretion whether any punishment at all should be imposed. It is both unusual and in general, in my opinion, undesirable that the court should not have a discretion in the imposition of penalties and sentences, for circumstances alter cases and it is a traditional function of a court of justice to endeavour to make the punishment appropriate to the circumstances as well as to the nature of the crime.

Let the punishment fit the crime — and the criminal. Parliament cannot do that in advance. It must be done in the court where all the evidence is presented and the arguments are made about the particular case.

The philosopher George Santayana said: 'Those who cannot remember the past are condemned to repeat it.' In 1883, well over a century ago, New South Wales introduced a mandatory sentencing scheme following pressure by the media. It was abandoned one year later because of the palpable injustice it caused. While the scheme was still in effect, the *Sydney Herald* editorial of 27 September 1883 said:

> We have the fact before us that in a case where a light penalty would have satisfied the claims of justice, the judge was prevented from doing what he believed to be right and was compelled to pass a sentence which he believed to be excessive, and therefore unjust, because the rigidity of the law left him no discretion.

One theory behind mandatory sentences of imprisonment for comparatively minor criminal offences is that of *selective incapacitation*. That generally means removing from the community minor offenders before they progress to major offences. It is assumed that most crimes in a given place are the work of a relatively small proportion of offenders and that if you can take them out of circulation at an early stage you can prevent the continuation and escalation of offending. This supports 'three strikes and you're in' laws, with increasing terms of imprisonment fixed in legislation.

But can the system identify, apprehend and detain for a sufficient time enough high-rate offenders at the right time in their criminal careers to substantially reduce the crime rate? Where is the evidence that it can? Will the effect really be, conversely, to put minor criminals into institutions where they learn to be major criminals more quickly than they would on the streets? One effect of such laws is known.

Prison populations surge. In California, where mandatory sentencing has taken a firm hold, it has been calculated that by 2002 the corrections budget required will be double the 1998 level of 9 per cent to 18 per cent of the overall state budget. Confoundingly, crime goes on. So should taxpayers be expected to bear the increased costs of policies that don't work?

And it cannot be denied that there is manifest injustice in a young Aborigine being gaoled for a year for stealing a packet of biscuits, a drunken Aborigine being gaoled for a month for stealing a towel from a Darwin clothesline or a destitute Californian black receiving a 25-year sentence for stealing a slice of pizza. (These are real cases.) In some Northern Territory cases there have been tragic consequences.

Mandatory sentences are otherwise supported because they are said to deter criminals; but criminal penalties are at best a blunt instrument in achieving deterrence and their effectiveness is not enhanced by simply making them heavier. Sharper and smarter means are required. The facts that crime goes on and the prison populations grow demonstrate that the penalties are not having a meaningful deterrent effect. A small but growing body of research confirms that conclusion. Crime rates have not been shown to be affected by the frequency of punishment or its severity; they are more responsive to intelligence-led policing, targeting specific areas, conduct or persons, and to overall improvements in social conditions.

Apart from increasing public expense, the dangers of mandatory sentencing include the following:

• *Adverse impact upon the independence of the judiciary.* Schemes of mandatory or grid sentences (see below) show a lack of confidence in the sentencing laws and procedures that have been in force for a very long time and, with the odd exception, have worked in a just and fair way. That undermines public confidence in the courts. It also puts the government's invisible hand on one side of the scales of justice before the scales are even used. The judge is not able any longer to act independently and impartially in a process that is clearly public before making a judgment to deprive a person of his or her liberty. Political pressure should not weigh upon the courts.

In the United States, where mandatory sentences (particularly for federal offences) are widespread, Chief Justice Rehnquist of the Supreme Court (not a Justice who is known to be 'soft' on crime) has said: 'These mandatory minimums impose unduly harsh punishment for first-time offenders and have led to an inordinate increase in the prison population.' Justice Kennedy of that court has said: 'Judges should not have their sentencing discretion controlled.'

- *Reduction in guilty pleas*. Over 95 per cent of criminal cases are resolved by pleas of guilty. There does not need to be a full hearing in those cases, enabling them to pass quickly through the courts. If that rate were to fall, the courts, already stretched, would not be able to cope. Mandatory sentencing, we know from experience, causes pleas of guilty to dry up, clogging the courts with increased backlogs of cases, increasing legal costs (on both sides), extending waiting times for hearings and increasing the prison remand population. Defendants are more willing to take a chance of a lucky acquittal some time in the future than accept a certain, unfairly harsh penalty immediately.

- *Increase of charge bargaining*. Charge bargaining (or plea bargaining) conversely increases, transferring the exercise of discretion from the courts (where it is visible and accountable) to prosecutors (where it is not). In order to move the cases along (so as to prevent unmanageable backlogs and pressures developing), prosecutors accept pleas to inappropriately less severe offences where there are not mandatory sentences. Such results quite naturally disappoint and offend victims of crime.

- *Unjust sentencing.* Mandatory sentences are imposed for offences that are committed, in the main, by disadvantaged members of society (such as Aborigines and black Americans cited earlier). Underprivileged sections of society are therefore unfairly discriminated against. Most offenders from disadvantaged groups are least likely to be able to afford competent legal representation. Studies have shown that mandatory sentences discriminate against Aborigines, women and children.

- *Lack of criminal justice system support.* Those involved in the criminal justice system will go to great lengths to avoid the impact of the mandatory provisions. None of the functionaries in the system sees merit in such sentences from his or her point of view, so none acts to support them. The criminal justice agencies are not populated by politicians, so those who work in them do what they can to avoid the consequences of mandatory provisions.

- *Danger to law enforcement.* Sentences of mandatory imprisonment create additional dangers for police (and others in the law enforcement chain), particularly if they are mandatory sentences for more serious offences. Desperate and violent criminals will take ruthless measures to avoid capture and punishment if they know that they are facing mandatory terms. There is no incentive to co-operate — and every incentive to beat or even kill a person who might end their liberty for a long fixed term.

In New South Wales there are mandatory life sentences prescribed for some cases of murder and drug trafficking. Those provisions were legislated as a result of political breast-beating. They have never been invoked because the courts have found (not surprisingly) that the pre-existing 'ordinary' discretionary sentencing provisions have been quite sufficient. Indeed, there are now over a dozen prisoners in New South Wales serving sentences from which they will never be released, sentences imposed by courts exercising their own discretion under laws that did not prescribe mandatory sentences.

A Senate Committee reported on the mandatory sentencing of juveniles in March 2000. It concluded that Northern Territory mandatory sentencing legislation as it affects juveniles contravenes Australia's international obligations. With respect to Western Australia, it concluded that the legislation also contravened those obligations, but in the practice less so. It suggested that more work be done on alternatives to mandatory sentencing (such as diversionary programs, victim conferencing and the development of judicial sentencing guidelines). It said: 'The Committee is convinced by the submissions and argument that mandatory minimum sentencing is not appropriate in a modern democracy that values human rights, and it contravenes the Convention on the Rights of the Child'. It accepted the view that to compare the Northern Territory and Western Australian mandatory sentencing regimes was to compare bad with bad and to try to prioritise badness.

* * *

'GRID' SENTENCES

An intermediate step between normal sentencing discretion and mandatory penalties is so-called 'grid' sentencing (or, in US parlance, 'sentencing guidelines' or 'matrix sentencing'). This is another favourite of the politicians, proven already in the United States to be productive of just as much injustice as mandatory sentences. The sentence to be imposed is plotted geometrically on a grid, having regard only to the description of the offence and the offender's past record. Little scope is given to the judge to move outside the box. No regard is had to the circumstances of the offence or the offender personally. This scheme produces the same vices as mandatory sentencing, particularly strengthening the hand of prosecutors to charge bargain an offender into another box in the grid. The voices of victims in the sentencing process become muted.

A system of this kind was allowed to develop in the United States where conditions are very different from ours. There are no appeals available against sentences, at least in the federal areas, and judges do not give the lengthy reasons for sentences that are given here and are able to be examined and criticised.

Judges in the United States are often elected to office and they react to the idiosyncratic demands of their electorates. That may not produce just and fair results for either the prisoners or the community. Elected judges sometimes seek to justify popular decisions that may even be contrary to law by saying that they are keeping in touch with the views of their constituents. Judges make such decisions, even knowing that an appeal court may overturn them. An American law professor has written (in relation to a particular judge acting that way):

By endorsing those judges who agree with them and removing those who do not, what benefit will accrue to the citizenry? Will their actions foster a more just system of justice? We all know that the opposite is true. A public that demands that judges rule in accordance with their wishes will have created a judiciary composed of judges who decide cases based on public pressure rather than on the rule of law and who rank job tenure above judicial independence. A justice system motivated by the public's intimidation and manipulation will reek of injustice. And that demanding public will be assured that the promise of equal justice under law is nothing but a motto chiselled on stone.

While the public's lack of appreciation of the importance of an independent judiciary may be understandable, a judge's is not. I'm saddened because the judge either does not grasp or chooses to ignore the single essential quality of the American justice system: detachment. As Justice Frankfurter explained,

> Courts are not representative bodies. They are not designed to be a good reflex of a democratic society . . . Their essential quality is detachment, founded on independence.

And I am saddened that the judge has accepted the authority of judicial office, but ignored the responsibility.

In parts of the United States where the unwanted burdens of the 'grid' approach to sentencing are heavily felt, some states have dealt with the problems by simply reducing the levels of sentences in the boxes. While that would seem to be defeating the expressed purposes of such a scheme, it clearly demonstrates its arbitrariness — not a desirable quality of any sentencing regime.

Grid systems are a boon for the bureaucrats, however. A vast administrative structure must be established to set the guidelines, keep them under review and administer their consequences.

DEATH PENALTY

It is fairly obvious that those who are in favour of the death penalty have more affinity with assassins than those who are not.

REMY DE GOURMONT

A lot of sentencing effort could be saved, of course, by the death penalty. It can be quick and cheap and certainly prevents the dead person from reoffending. It could thus be described as the perfect individual deterrent (but only after the crime has been committed) and, of course, only if the right person is killed. What if our less than perfect criminal justice system makes a mistake and the wrong person is killed, someone who did not need to be deterred? That sort of damage is very hard to undo. It happens in places where the death penalty is applied and it happened when we had it in Australia. In the United States in January 2000, the Governor of Illinois referred to his own state's 'shameful record of convicting innocent people' and ordered a moratorium on executions. That state alone has exonerated 13 death row inmates since 1976 (in which time there have been 12 executions). Nationwide since 1973, 87 prisoners have been released from death row after new evidence pointed to their innocence; in 8 cases DNA evidence established it conclusively. A project centred in New York, called the Innocence Project, re-examines DNA evidence from past cases. It has led since 1993 to the release of over 70 people from prison and death row.

There are only two real purposes served by the death penalty and neither is a legitimate one. The first is the enabling of those who administer it — the politicians who set it up — to tell us all how tough they are by having the power of life and death over us (but not personally, of course, someone else does the dirty work). They equate toughness with brutality and a selective disregard for the facts. The second is revenge — payback — at its most primitive. Can that ever be sufficient justification for official murder?

Any taking of a human life is the ultimate abuse of human rights. Consequently there need to be extraordinarily compelling reasons for doing so by official action. Such reasons are not to be found in the idea that the death penalty deters likeminded offenders from committing similar offences. It doesn't, as study after study has shown. United States Attorney General, Janet Reno, has said: 'I have inquired for most of my adult life about studies that might show that the death penalty is a deterrent, and I have not seen any research that would substantiate that point.'

The death penalty is usually prescribed for offences of the most dramatic kind, such as terrorism, murder and drug trafficking on an enormous scale. The people likely to commit such offences do not pause to consider the consequences. Terrorists are resigned to death for the cause. Murderers act, usually, at the height of irrational passion (less often in cold blood, but in those cases they take a calculated risk that they will not be caught). Drug tsars do not expect to be identified, much less charged and prosecuted. The death penalty is not a deterrent.

If the death penalty is really intended to deter people from offending, why not impose it on traffic offenders? For those types of offences we would see a true general deterrent effect (and the safest and least congested roads in the world).

The death penalty is opposed by the United Nations, the

European Union and the Pope (amongst many others). Australia has abolished it. Let's not go backwards. Some say that a plebiscite would result in a majority favouring capital punishment for some offences: so it might; but a majority might also vote for a government handout of $1000 for every citizen. Responsible public policy is not made that way.

SENTENCING GUIDELINE JUDGMENTS

In the middle part of 1998, with the customary law and order auction beginning to warm up before the March 1999 election, there was talk of legislation directing judges to sentence in particular ways: mandatory sentences, mandatory minimum sentences, grid sentences, and so on; somewhat in the ways of Western Australia and the Northern Territory. The most strident calls came from the opposition. The government searched for ways to appease the demagogues while at the same time demonstrating 'toughness' on crime. The NSW Chief Justice looked for a way out of all this, favouring judicial self-regulation.

On a visit to England the Chief Justice lighted upon the system of guideline judgments that had been in operation there for 20 years or more, prior to the UK *Crime and Disorder Act 1998*. While the NSW Government cobbled together the Criminal Procedure Amendment (Sentencing Guidelines) Bill 1998, providing (in a fashion) for a scheme whereby the appellate court could be required by the government to set guidelines, the Court of Criminal Appeal prepared instead to institute its own regime, based on the English model, of producing guideline judgments for sentences in particular categories of offence. The principal objective was to ensure consistency in sentencing between courts and judges — structuring, not restricting, discretion.

Individualised justice must still be able to be done while *equal justice* is pursued. What do I mean by that? Equal justice means that a wildly reckless drunken driver who runs down and kills a child on a pedestrian crossing and a submissive woman who in a fit of despair stabs with a kitchen knife and kills the aggressive husband who has beaten her and made her life a misery for years are both liable to be convicted of the offence of manslaughter and the same legal rules will apply to both at all stages of the proceedings. Individualised justice means that the courts considering what penalties to impose following such convictions will be able to take all the circumstances of the offences and the offenders — their conduct and history — into account before fashioning suitable sentences, and not simply look up the prescribed penalty for manslaughter and apply the same sentence in both cases.

The NSW Chief Justice has stated:

> Unless judges are able to mould the sentence to the circumstances of the individual case then, irrespective of how much legislative forethought has gone into the determination of a particular regime, there will always be the prospect of injustice. No judge of my acquaintance is prepared to tolerate becoming an instrument of injustice. Guideline judgments are preferable to the constraints of mandatory minimum terms or grid sentencing.

Guideline judgments began in the 1970s in the English Court of Appeal, intended to give authoritative guidance to trial judges in sentencing for certain offences. A guideline judgment goes beyond the sentencing for the particular case or cases before the court. It suggests a scale of sentences, an appropriate starting point or a list of relevant considerations (all three approaches have been adopted) for the type of crime before the court, identifying aggravating or mitigating circumstances to be considered in individual cases. The guidelines are not meant to be applied rigidly to every case; they are for assistance only; the sentencing judge retains the discretion or freedom to move within or from the guidelines. The reasons for any departure from the guidelines must be explained in a judgment. Sentences in guideline judgments are indicators, just as maximum penalties prescribed by Parliament are indicators.

Guideline judgments go some way towards correcting the unfortunate and erroneous impression, driven by the media's concentration on specific instances of unusually light sentences, that sentences in general are too lenient. By labelling such judgments as *guideline judgments*, the guidance given by superior courts in such matters becomes more apparent to all concerned and to the public.

Late in 1998 the NSW Chief Justice signalled the court's intention to formulate guideline judgments in appropriate cases and moves were made to identify a suitable starting category of offence. Dangerous driving causing death or grievous bodily harm was singled out, because of a history of a large number of Crown appeals against the inadequacy of sentences for those offences and because of some apparent inconsistency of approach by sentencing judges. (It also happened to be a category of crime about which the media commentators had been particularly strident for some time.)

The Court of Criminal Appeal issued the first guideline judgment for New South Wales in the case of *Jurisic* on 12 October 1998. It provided a starting point for dangerous driving offences with certain fairly common characteristics that were described in the judgment.

The second category of offence identified by the court for a guideline judgment was armed robbery. The judgments in those cases (*Henry* and others) were delivered on 12 May 1999 and set a range of sentences for cases with certain described characteristics.

The first Commonwealth guideline judgment hearing was held on 30 July 1999 for the offence of being knowingly concerned in the importation of prohibited drugs. Judgment was delivered on 16 December 1999.

The next category of state offence to be identified was break, enter and steal, heard on 1 October 1999 (judgment also delivered on 16 December 1999 in which a collection of relevant considerations was described). The next was heard on 12 May 2000, a hearing on the sentence discount to be given for a plea of guilty. Judgment was delivered on 17 August 2000.

Since the first guideline judgment in *Jurisic*, there has been a marked change in sentencing practice. Sentencing judges, with only very few exceptions, have applied the guidelines in cases of dangerous driving causing death or grievous bodily harm. In the few cases where Crown appeals have since been required, it would appear that the judges involved have perhaps been testing the limits of the operation of the guidelines.

There has been a blessed relief from the hysterical and uninformed outpourings of the media, for which we should all be grateful. As I have noted above, the exceptional cases usually attract the most publicity and if exceptions resulting from judicial error can be eliminated we shall all be better served.

There came into existence during all this the *Criminal Procedure Amendment (Sentencing Guidelines) Act* which seeks to alter the effect of the 1998 Act by permitting the DPP to intervene independently in proceedings brought by the Attorney General to, amongst other things, 'inform the court with respect to any relevant pending appeal with respect to sentence'. The effect of this amending legislation, in reality, is to cast the burden of the conduct of guideline appeals under the Act (in addition to those under the court scheme) onto the DPP. *Noblesse oblige*, I suppose . . .

The reaction of the judiciary to community concerns by way of self-regulation is unobjectionable and should be supported. The court's regime of guideline judgments, notwithstanding its teething troubles, is completely acceptable in principle. However, we need to scrutinise very carefully any attempt by the executive to have the court do its bidding in ways that may infringe its independence. We also need to be careful to ensure that measures taken do not result in unfairness to any of the parties involved or to future litigants.

The danger is in the myth that Parliament can in some way take the place of the courts by sentencing criminals in advance of their crimes. Parliament's proper role is to set maximum penalties and alternatives — caps on how high the courts can go and other courses they can take. It is then for the courts to do justice fairly — and sometimes with mercy.

Nine: The Island Continent

No man is an Island, entire of itself;
every man is a piece of the Continent,
a part of the main.

JOHN DONNE

People like people like them.

PAULINE HANSON

Nor is an island continent entire of itself, even if we don't like some of the people elsewhere who are not exactly like us. We live in a shrinking world.

There is a popular myth that there are other people — foreign people — trying to tell us what to do in our own country. The United Nations, it is said, through its various committees wants to impose rules on us from afar and make us do things that we don't want to do.

This myth surfaces sometimes in confused and unexpected ways. For example, New South Wales, Victoria and the Australian Capital Territory proposed to conduct trials of safe injecting premises for heroin addicts. By doing so, they were seeking to follow a course set by the Netherlands, Switzerland, Germany and Spain, a course that would enable individual jurisdictions to tailor their own programs for dealing best with their own problems of drug abuse. After quite an interval the Prime Minister arose and declared that such trials could breach Australia's international obligations and that they should be put on hold. He was referring to a letter he had seen from the International Narcotics Control Board, the administrative body set up to oversee the operation of the 1961 international Single Convention on Narcotic Drugs (to which Australia became a party in 1968). Was Australia being dictated to by an international body?

The NSW Special Minister for State apparently thought so and promptly retorted: 'An international agency should not be dictating Australian policies' (setting the scene for yet another Commonwealth/State stoush).

But hang on a minute! Australia voluntarily became and remains a party to the convention, which does not in its terms prevent properly controlled clinical trials of the type contemplated for medical research purposes. The state and territory parliaments have legislated for them — in the case of New South Wales after a much-publicised Drug Summit. Who is making policy? State and territory governments or an international body through its influence on the Commonwealth?

Australia is but one nation in about 190 in a global community that is ever shrinking — whose borders and lines of division are being blurred and rendered ineffective as time goes by. This blurring is reflected in the nature of crimes that are now being committed across the old boundaries and in the ways in which those crimes now have to be fought. We cannot ignore what is happening elsewhere; we are affected by events in other parts of the globe in ways that we cannot control but to which we must react. And despite our small population and our isolated position, we do not like to be ignored in the global community. Or exploited by others.

But power to influence others carries with it obligations. If we want to exercise power and to be respected internationally, we are obliged to observe the conditions that are set for us, with our agreement, by the international community. Note that the actions we take are of our own free will and after due consideration. We are not forced into anything. That obligation also carries over into our law making and law enforcement, including our criminal law.

Laws do not just spring from the womb of Parliament fully formed and perfect. The process of making laws is quite complex. (Some argue that in our representative democracy it should be even more complex, to ensure greater input from those the laws will affect.) For the most part laws evolve. That process is a continuing one. We inherited our law from England in a job lot, but we now change and add to it as circumstances require and we have moved some distance from the motherland in many things. Rarely do circumstances change so dramatically that a whole new set of laws needs to be made in one hit. The GST is an example of such a change, and wartime created a need for special new provisions.

The evolution of laws occurs in a conservative way, usually a little behind the demands of the most vocal sections of the community. As that evolution occurs, the law makers must have regard to the facts and circumstances that presently exist, to the changes that are likely to occur in the future, to the policies of the government in power, to the existing laws, to past regulation, to the relationship the new laws must have with other existing provisions and practices, to the relations between the states and territories and the Commonwealth, and to international laws and standards.

Why? What have provisions affecting other countries got to do with us? Some ask why we should pay any attention at all to what comes out of a meeting hall at the United Nations, for instance. To answer that question we need to look back — and forward.

Looking back we see that the history of humankind has been a story of conflict and struggle, with the odd shining moment visible through the smoke, dust and pain. We know from bitter experience that if people in positions of power are not controlled by the rule of law, they will make us suffer. Those of us who are fortunate enough to live in relative comfort in stable societies with well-established controls of that kind, forget that even today, without those controls, despots are making life a misery for the majority of their subjects: the former Yugoslavia (until recently), Burma, North Korea, Angola, the Congo and Iraq come readily to mind. East Timor has just emerged from under the Indonesian jackboot. In the recent past Rwanda, Albania, Iran and South Africa have suffered. Dictators in Germany, Spain, Italy, Russia and Japan acted atrociously before and during World War II. And so it goes on, back through the pages of history as societies struggle to achieve and then maintain the just rule of law.

Throughout history, from at least the Middle Ages, there have been attempts to prevent such outrages, or at least to lessen their impact. The aftermath of World War II finally persuaded the nations of the world to take effective action. One of the brightest moments following the creation of the United Nations was the 1948 Universal Declaration of Human Rights. It is not a long document and it is reproduced as an appendix for easy reference. Read it. Is it not simply a statement of the minimum rights that you would like to enjoy? What do we have to fear from enforcing such a document — from putting into practice the principles there set out?

The big issue for all nations is how to guarantee those

minimum rights — and other economic, cultural and social rights found in other instruments — to all their citizens. Australia does pretty well, overall (although it could do a lot better for Aborigines and Torres Strait Islanders and for *genuine* refugees).

Looking forward we see that the world is shrinking. The global village is upon us. Every day millions of people routinely cross national borders, including our own. We Australians are great international travellers. Each (non-Olympic Games) year 2 million airline passengers land in Australia. Up to 40 000 of them are new arrivals who stay. Television brings the world into our living rooms. We can connect with it instantaneously via the Internet and e-mail. (Australia is the fifth most connected country.) We have been watching foreign TV programs since television began here and listening to the world by radio for a long time before. We are influenced in all that we do by what we know is happening in other countries.

The law is not exempt from such influences and they will only strengthen in the future.

Since the Universal Declaration of Human Rights, many kinds of international instruments have been developed — covenants, conventions, declarations, standards, protocols — on a large range of subjects, affecting the kinds of policies that should be adopted and laws that should be made by nations, such as Australia, that are parties to them. We have also had a major part in the creation of many of them, ever since the time of the first president of the UN General Assembly in 1948, an Australian, Dr H. V. ('Doc') Evatt.

Australia has adopted such instruments as treaties and solemn agreements, which we have promised to keep by observing their terms when making and enforcing policy and laws within Australia (including the states and territories), and when taking action in the relevant areas.

So there are at least four good reasons why we should observe the terms of such instruments:

1   They are binding agreements upon us as a nation that we should not lightly break, the world having watched us make them and expecting that we will carry them out.

2   The making of such agreements is a representation by our government to us that the government will comply with them.

3   They are documents that prescribe standards, usually minimum standards, for the conduct of all people and which therefore should be supported in the hope that not only will they do us some good, but they may also help to prevent some of the horrors of the past being repeated elsewhere. If governments disposed to abuse their populations see that the rest of the world is observing these standards and expects them to do likewise, they might reluctantly follow suit (at least to a greater extent than might otherwise be the case). This is called leading by example, something that Australia, unfortunately, has not always been disposed to do.

4   They can make government easier. Humankind sets ideals for itself, goals to which we collectively aspire (peace, freedom, democracy, prosperity, health, education, clean earth, air and water and so on). If those in power are seen to share those aspirations or hopes, they are more likely to have popular support for policies and actions of their own that are directed towards those (and perhaps other) ends. There is less likelihood of opposition to the rules that they lay down for our conduct. Even less crime (maybe).

The creation of international instruments by the UN and other international bodies prescribing standards for us to observe is *not* a case of others dictating to us what we should do. We are involved in the decision-making process; we go into it with our eyes open; we contribute to the creation of these instruments and the bodies set up to monitor them and we make the choice to accept the result and to observe the requirements set. It serves our purposes to do so.

AN ILLUSTRATION

Is genocide a crime? Think about it . . . genocide!

No, not against Australian law!

It is not a crime against our inherited English common law or against any law of Australia. The Federal Court recently confirmed that to be the case. The result is that if a person commits genocide — anywhere, even in Australia — he or she cannot be prosecuted for that offence in Australia.

However, there is an international Convention on the Prevention and Punishment of the Crime of Genocide (1948). The convention makes genocide a crime against customary international law and imposes obligations on the parties to the convention to prosecute or extradite offenders. That is one result of the UN initiatives to which I have referred.

And yes, Australia is a party to the convention and has been for 30 years. Before and now under the convention, Australia was and is obliged to extradite any person who appears to have committed the crime elsewhere back to the place where it was committed. But Australia has never enacted the convention into domestic law, so it is not part of the law of Australia and a prosecution here for genocide is not possible.

The convention remains for Australia just another treaty, in this case a broken promise to the world. It would be a simple breach to heal: all that is required is a very short Act of the federal Parliament.

ANOTHER ILLUSTRATION

Mandatory sentencing (again). In all parts of Australia there are mandatory penalties prescribed for some offences. For example, fines of fixed amounts are set for traffic offences. They are mandatory — the regulators and the courts must impose the penalties that are prescribed. There is no discretion to move within a range of possible penalties.

But mandatory imprisonment is another matter; and it is only in the Northern Territory and Western Australia that there is mandatory sentencing to imprisonment for comparatively minor offences (those that would be dealt with elsewhere by fines, recognisances, diversionary schemes or suspended sentences). The laws themselves are bad, but in those two jurisdictions they are worse because of the discriminatory way in which they work against Aborigines, juveniles and women.

Australia is a party to the International Covenant on Civil and Political Rights (ICCPR). It signed up voluntarily, years ago. It is also a party to the First Optional Protocol to the ICCPR (that is, not compulsory) which established the UN Human Rights Committee. Individuals may petition the Committee to examine claims of official human rights abuses once all domestic avenues have been exhausted.

A bit of history. Tasmania once had laws that made criminal homosexual intercourse between consenting adults in private. It refused to change the laws and appeals all the way to the High Court were unsuccessful (as they were bound to be, given the state of the law). A Tasmanian man petitioned the Human Rights Committee which declared that the laws infringed his human rights. The Committee cannot tell Australia what to do, but Australia (the Commonwealth) has agreed to be part of the regime in which the Human Rights Committee operates and listened to what was said. Australia passed laws invalidating the Tasmanian laws.

Another bit of history. The Northern Territory once had a law enabling euthanasia to occur in strictly controlled circumstances. Australia (the Commonwealth) legislated to make it unlawful, overturning the Territory law.

And some more history. Victoria had a law limiting the availability of IVF programs. It was overturned by the Federal Court. The Commonwealth Government announced its intention to legislate to restore the limitations.

Recently Australia made one of its regular reports to the UN Committee (although late). The issue of mandatory sentencing was debated. The Committee urged the Commonwealth to legislate to abolish the procedures in the Northern Territory and Western Australia (which it can do, of course).

This time the Commonwealth reacted by denigrating the Committee and the UN and proclaiming that neither governs Australia. The Northern Territory Chief Minister stated that the Committee's views are not consistent with the Northern Territory electorate's wishes. Maybe not, but does that make the Committee wrong or mean that it is acting beyond its powers — powers endorsed by Australia? Is that a reason for ignoring the Committee's views? (Did anyone ask the views of Tasmanians before the Commonwealth legislated that time?)

OUR RECORD

In some other cases we have not been so slow to honour our promises. A number of international instruments have been enacted as Schedules to the *Human Rights and Equal Opportunity Commission Act 1986* and so have some application in the law of Australia. These include the Discrimination (Employment and Occupation) Convention; the International Covenant on Civil and Political Rights (ICCPR); the Declaration of the Rights of the Child; the Declaration on the Rights of Mentally Retarded Persons; and the Declaration on the Rights of Disabled Persons. We quickly adopted the Convention on the Rights of the Child; and we are a party to many more, including (as I have said) the First Optional Protocol to the ICCPR. But since 1997 particularly, we have withdrawn from active human rights diplomacy and cooperation with UN human rights bodies.

In the criminal law, chiefly by coincidence, we have incorporated most of the major provisions of the international instruments into our own procedures. They include the principles that:

- people are to be treated equally before the law;
- in our courts everyone is entitled to a fair and public hearing by a competent, independent and impartial judiciary;
- all persons charged with criminal offences are presumed to be innocent until proven guilty according to law; and
- people are to be tried fairly and without undue delay (although we could do better with that one).

Again, there is nothing to fear from adherence to such international instruments. They merely prescribe standards that we would want to observe for ourselves, and we adopt them by choice. We do not torture suspects in order to obtain confessions. We do not give our police unlimited powers to deal with crime as they see fit. We do not punish children as we punish adults.

Sometimes international instruments can have indirect consequences. The Franklin Dam case in the High Court preserved the lower Gordon River in Tasmania. That decision resulted from the enforcement by the High Court of international instruments to which Australia is a party. We would not have had the ground-breaking Mabo decision without recognition of international standards applying to indigenous peoples. The Tasmanian legislation making criminal sexual acts between consenting adult males in private was over-ridden by reliance on other international benchmarks.

These and other decisions have also operated as controls on the unfettered use of power by those in authority. Decision makers will stop to think of the possible consequences if action is contemplated that may breach accepted international norms and instruments to which Australia has become a party. In more recent times we have been relying on international instruments to incorporate into our law the standards they prescribe, where that is necessary to resolve an ambiguity or to fill a gap in our own law. That practice has become well established in the higher Australian courts and elsewhere in the Commonwealth.

But . . . unfortunately, Australia's history of the observance of the international obligations it has incurred has been uneven, even patchy. Could there be some politics at play here? Or some odd ideas about the nature of leadership?

In his complaints about trials of safe injecting premises the Prime Minister was displaying selectivity in the international instruments that he would choose to observe. Are they a bit like election promises — core and non-core? If so, which is which, or aren't we to know until some political advantage is seen in declaring a position?

The Prime Minister seems to be able to conveniently overlook Australia's international obligations. Australia has failed to comply with the following instruments:

- *International Covenant on Civil and Political Rights*. The mandatory sentencing regimes in place in the Northern Territory and Western Australia are in direct breach of provisions of the Covenant.
- *Convention on the Rights of the Child*. Again, these mandatory sentencing regimes are in breach of this instrument.
- *Convention on the Prevention and Punishment of the Crime of Genocide*. Not put into effect, as noted earlier.
- *Convention Against All Forms of Racial Discrimination*. In March 1999 a UN committee found that the *Native Title Amendment Act* infringed the convention. The Commonwealth Government thumbed its nose. Mr Howard said at the time: 'Australian laws are made by Australian parliamentarians elected by the Australian people, not by UN committees.'
- *Convention Relative to the Status of Refugees*. Ours is the only developed country that imprisons refugees from persecution.
- *International Labour Organisation conventions*. An international committee of experts in 1998 said Australia's federal industrial relations laws breached international conventions on collective bargaining. The Minister for Workplace Relations dismissed the criticism as incorrect and gratuitous.

• *European Union*. In 1997 Australia refused to include a standard human rights clause in a framework trade agreement.

In an interview with John Laws in December 1999 the Prime Minister said:

> You can ignore your obligations under an international treaty if you choose to. The reason why you can ignore them is because in the end there is no sanction against you. Other than the sanction of being seen as having potentially breached some agreement that you have signed.

So it's OK to break an agreement you have made, as long as there will be no punishment. And it doesn't matter if others think you won't keep your word. What kind of a message does that send, Mr Howard? Oh great leader . . .

But, to be fair, both sides of politics seem to have the same facility when it comes to international obligations. The Keating Government took the view that when it ratified an international treaty it was just sending a signal to the international community. Australians had no right to expect a treaty to be respected unless a local law was passed.

And what of concerns for those trials of safe injecting premises? Well, Mr Howard had hitched his wagon to the letter from the International Narcotics Control Board. What did the letter say? Only (reportedly) that the board was 'extremely sceptical' about the value of clinical trials and that it believed that injecting rooms were 'the wrong way to go', but not that they would be in breach of the convention.

It is not the job of the board to dictate policy to governments. Government opinions have precedence over the views of the board. The NSW Special Minister for State should have discovered that and been comforted by it. Mr Howard must have known that, yet he chose to represent the situation otherwise. It seems that the Prime Minister, not one to observe international agreements unless he chooses to, had chosen for his own short-term political purposes to be dictated to by an international body that did not even have the power to do so.

A BILL OF RIGHTS

Even without the implementation of attitudes of the kind displayed by the Prime Minister (or 'Prime Miniature' as some would have it), Australia is becoming increasingly isolated from its legal foundations and must more actively set about securing its own. As I have noted, our legal and constitutional traditions came from England. But since then there have been developments in both countries that have set our law increasingly apart from the English common law as it has continued to evolve in that country and in similar jurisdictions (Canada, New Zealand, South Africa). And when we are confronted by new questions and seek precedents for ways in which to answer them we often cannot adopt them from other places. The United States, a country with a legal system modelled substantially on English common law, has had a constitutional Bill of Rights for a couple of hundred years. Canada has had a constitutionally entrenched Charter of Rights and Freedoms since 1982. New Zealand has had a statutory bill of rights (the *Bill of Rights Act*) since 1990. South Africa has a constitutional Bill of Rights. The United Kingdom now has come under the European Convention (with the *Human Rights Act* 1998). Those instruments guide the application and development of the laws of those countries away from the traditions to which we still adhere and upon which we have built. We cannot follow because we do not have a bill of rights. Our High Court struggles to 'discover' rights for us when we need them (and gets a public walloping every time it does so).

Most democracies now have some kind of statement of the fundamental rights of their citizens somewhere in their laws, often in their constitutions. Australia and its states do not. We are the last major developed common law country not to have a bill of rights.

Certainty is preferable, especially in the criminal law, although we can't always enjoy it. A bill of rights that spells out the rights we should all enjoy under the law would provide greater certainty, and less opportunity for criticism by talkback radio or anybody else.

We need a bill of rights. Preferably it should be constitutionally entrenched. Such a step would be entirely consistent with the modern international trend in legal development, but what odds are there of Australia following suit?

Ten: Future Directions

The future is made of the same stuff as the present.

SIMONE WEIL

(But what we do with that 'stuff' now will make a difference later.)

In his challenging book *Turning Point: Australians Choosing their Future* (Macmillan, 1999), Hugh Mackay (in a chapter titled Control — Should We Lock Everyone Up and Be Done With It?) writes about us as an anxious and insecure society wanting to get everything in our lives back in control. As a group we live with an undercurrent of fear which is well known to, and shamelessly exploited by, the politicians. They are not alone, of course. The media (including talkback) and commercial interests line up with them at every opportunity. This is obviously not the 'relaxed and comfortable' society that John Howard said he would like to see and which most of us would like to enjoy.

In many respects this is an uncertain age (but possibly no more uncertain than most past 'ages'). If that uncertainty in our minds is exaggerated into belief that the controls on society have broken down, that we are headed for anarchy and exploitation, then it is an easy next step to embrace 'toughness' and the empty rhetoric of law and order as the salvation. We are constantly given a helping hand in that direction by those who get a great deal of our attention — talkback radio for most of the time and politicians at election time. It suits their purposes. Nick Ross was talking about the United Kingdom, but he might as well have been talking about Australia when he said: 'We're barking mad about crime in this country. We have an obsession with believing the worst, conning ourselves that there was a golden age — typically 40 years before the one we're living in.'

Let us, instead, step aside from self-delusion, fear and prejudice and think about the situation in a reasoned way. And let us not uncritically accept the law and order agenda set by others; there are larger principles at stake. Of course we can always improve on what we have; but to do that we must challenge orthodoxies (accepted wisdom) and base intelligent thinking on the lessons of experience, our history. It is often easy to be wise after the event; it requires a bit more thought to be wise before it; even more to be able to prevent or avoid events that are undesirable.

QUO VADIS? WHERE ARE YOU — AND WE — GOING?

If we really want to reduce the undesirable — criminal — events that occur in our society and to deal effectively with their consequences, we need to change direction. At present we are trying to achieve those ends from the back end of the criminal process; that is, tackling the problems from the wrong end. We are ignoring the lessons that are there for us to see and apply in order to prevent the problems arising.

The Victorian-era Parramatta Gaol was closed a few years

ago and became a tourist attraction ('Look son, this is how prisoners were treated in the olden days!'). New South Wales Premier, Bob Carr, declared it unfit for human habitation. In November 1998, because of overcrowding in prisons, it was reopened as a working prison, Mr Carr proclaiming 'Serious offenders are going to gaol and they are spending longer in gaol. I make no apologies for that.' But it's nothing to be proud of, either. In 1999 and 2000, new prisons were announced for Kempsey and Windsor.

We find ourselves caught in a spiral of expensive punishment of offenders through the unchanged operation of the courts, the legal system and prisons, and of compensation for victims, which is now a big budget item, maybe $150 million a year in New South Wales. Nobody goes back to the beginning of the criminal process to see sensibly if a real change there might be more effective (and might save them from a lot of wind).

Our current path is an increasingly costly one and an increasingly futile one. By tackling the problem from the wrong end — by expenditure on the 'undertakers' — that bill can only increase without much general improvement to show for it.

FRONT END

We should start, instead, by addressing the origin of problems — at the front end. We know from other societies and common sense tells us that if the sick (including drug addicts) and disadvantaged are provided with proper public support, the chances of their becoming criminals are drastically reduced. Call it 'front-end resourcing'; putting some of the money that would otherwise be spent on the 'undertakers' into programs of public activities before those undertakers are needed.

How many ways can I say that? Is it not a self-evidently sensible way of reducing all our problems in the long term? But it requires persistence — determination over a period that is likely to be longer than one term of Parliament.

The futility of our present approach — cleaning up after the problem, rather than trying to prevent it in the first place — can be further illustrated. In the 1999 NSW state election additional funds were promised for police. They needed them anyway just to maintain services at something like the existing level, but the extra funds were earmarked to take more offenders off the streets and into the courts. The prosecutors were given a few dollars more, it was said, to be able to meet the additional workload (but they were already a good deal behind the current pace and already had a lot of catching up to do). So the police set off to put even more people into the bucket of offenders, a bucket that the prisons had to take over after the prosecutors and the courts had finished with it. (Unfortunately, the police have been filling the bucket faster than Corrective Services has been able to empty it.) The point is that the bucket can be as full as we like to make it. And zero tolerance policing, for example, would make it overflow in no time at all. Instead we should be looking for acceptable ways to empty it.

THE SYSTEM

The criminal justice system is just that — a 'system'. It operates by the interaction of many agencies and individuals at all the stages of a person's progress through the gateways to which I have referred earlier. The players interconnect at different times and at different points, but each institution has its own structure, functions, rules, procedures, accountability and, importantly, priorities and jealousies. They do not share these with each other. But a system can only deliver a high-quality outcome if the individual players do their own jobs as best they can (and not try to do each other's) and connect with each other effectively.

In New South Wales the criminal justice system costs more than $2 billion of public money per year (nearly 9 per cent of the state's expenditure). It involves the Police Service, the Attorney General's Department (which administers the courts and a number of other services), the Office of the DPP, Legal Aid Commission and Public Defenders, Juvenile Justice, the private legal profession (barristers and solicitors, where public money is also spent), Corrective Services and others. Even the Health Department is involved, administering medical science services for the courts (like DNA testing).

But each of those agencies has its own bit of turf, its own priorities. The police are under pressure to prevent and clear up crime, the prosecutors to get convictions (although our performance is not measured in those terms), the courts to dispose of as many cases as possible, the prisons to protect us from offenders (at least). The Health Department doesn't give too high a priority to court work; its job is to treat the sick.

What links these agencies? What brings them together in the 'system'? Certainly not any dedication to the task of achieving justice in the criminal process (although that may be an internal priority for one or two of them and for parts of others). Rather, it seems that they are simply thrown against each other at the various stages of a person's progress through the gateways from charge to imprisonment, and have to find ways to connect, while keeping the financial and other costs of doing so at the lowest level achievable. Often it is not a high priority to make that connection or to make it an effective one: for example, DNA comparison is the most potent crime-fighting tool available, better than fingerprints, yet those services have a very low order of priority in the Health Department which supplies them. Again, in the adversarial nature of our proceedings, while the prosecution (DPP) is in pursuit of the truth in a contested hearing, that is the last thing the defender of a 'guilty' accused person wants to assist in establishing.

Yet these agencies cannot do their work in the system without the contribution of the others. It is odd that there should still be such divisions between their 'turfs' and barriers between their operations.

RESOURCING

Because these agencies are 'running on empty' in most cases, each of them is after more from the available financial pie, so as to make its daily tasks more effective. The system in New South Wales (and perhaps to almost the same extent elsewhere) is running at the point of breakdown and has been for some time. This means that the overall priority for these agencies becomes not to cooperate with each other and share operational priorities, not to do their jobs to the highest possible standard, but merely to survive, to keep going with a semblance of effectiveness. Some 'non-core' functions have been redeployed or dispensed with altogether and it is likely that more will go. Reports on the operation of agencies become distorted; a positive spin has to be put on what has been able to be achieved with the resources available.

In New South Wales funds have been progressively squeezed from the criminal justice agencies and diverted elsewhere (one suspects including the Olympic Games). There is also an irrational commitment by the NSW Government to being debt free, which keeps overall public spending at too low a level to provide necessary services to the standard we expect. With resources at such low levels and demands on services increasing budgets are simply blowing out. In 1998–99 the NSW Police Service exceeded its budget by $58.4 million (an amount greater than the entire budget for the DPP). Corrective Services exceeded its budget by $33 million. Perhaps the overall pie is shrinking; perhaps tax revenue (the public purse) is just not great enough to provide public services at a level that we are entitled to enjoy. If that is so, how has it come about?

We have been taught by public commentators (and others) that 'big government' is inefficient and bad, so less money has been provided to it. We are told that lower government spending is good. Services have been privatised. And we have enjoyed the lower taxes that have resulted. (So we are told!)

At the same time, however, governments (indeed, politicians on all sides) and the media have been telling us that more law and order is good. Who provides that but government? It is, in fact, a core activity of government, something that it cannot privatise. The Hon. L J King AC, QC, former Chief Justice of South Australia, wrote recently in the *Australian Law Journal*:

> [The administration of justice] is not an optional extra which may be expanded or contracted according to economic circumstances. If, for lack of resources, justice cannot be delivered efficiently and expeditiously, the government is failing in one of the very purposes for which organised society exists.

But government can't pay for it (and that is why people may be turning to inadequately regulated private security arrangements). Perhaps the shortage of public funds is the reason why the 'solutions' put forward by governments are the immediately cheaper options — more police powers, longer sentences and more prisons (forgetting the other players and forgetting the short-sightedness of such policies which become expensive in the long term). But even those options cost some money up front . . .

Whatever the real cause of the budget squeezes, it has meant that chief executive officers in the criminal justice system have become experts in crisis management. They are required constantly to work on the just-in-time principle. There is no capacity to make forward plans, to explore the savings that might emerge from greater cooperation between agencies in the system or to give adequate attention to matters before the very last possible moment. This is no way to run a government and it cannot continue forever without a crisis or a severe drop in standards (or both). We deserve better than that.

To take a more specific example from the criminal justice system: my prosecutors are flat out, not being able to commence work on trials until the day before they begin. There is then a mighty time-consuming contest in court, involving enormous cost and the time and involvement of so many people (police, witnesses and victims, jurors, court staff, judges, lawyers, etc.). With just a small increase in our budget (probably about 10 per cent, a mere drop from the Olympic bucket), prosecutors would have the time to look at matters in advance, to make sure the evidence is complete and notified fully and earlier to the defence, to discuss issues with the defence and see just what is in dispute, to refine the charges if necessary — all with the result of more pleas of guilty and shorter trials for those that do continue, confined to issues that are genuinely in dispute. If we could do that, there would be substantial long-term savings to the system as a whole, a higher level of professional service and a good deal lower level of stress for all involved.

Front-end resourcing! It has already been shown to work at the preliminary stages in the Magistrates' Courts, if legal aid can be made available to enable defendants to be given realistic advice before the criminal justice juggernaut — that great Rolls Royce of a trial process through all the gateways to which I have referred — heads off with them aboard down that long and costly highway.

Take an individual case: a young man, unhappy at the ending of a relationship with a young woman, doused her in petrol and set her alight. Miraculously, she survived, but with appalling disabilities. She returned to her family in England. The man was charged with attempted murder. There was no real dispute that he had done what he did but he pleaded not guilty. To prove the case, it was necessary to bring the victim back for the trial — such are the requirements of our system. She came back, at great cost to the public and huge pain and discomfort to herself and inconvenience to her support person. And on the first day of the trial? The man pleaded guilty. It was no longer necessary to hold a trial and it was no longer necessary for the woman to be here.

The man was relying on his 'right to silence' and all that entails. He did what he was legally entitled to do, but where was the justice in the outcome? The victim was made to suffer yet again. The man lost any benefit by way of reduction of sentence that he could have earned by cooperating with the trial process and pleading guilty at an earlier time. The community (the taxpayer) paid the financial costs.

Events like that are an unnecessary burden on the resources of the agencies involved. Legislation could prevent such an event occurring again. The defence could be forced to disclose matters and to make a meaningful contribution to the resolution of the trial process at an earlier stage. More front-end resourcing, of effort and application, and of money.

The NSW Government has foreshadowed legislation that will require greater defence disclosure and cooperation in the prosecution process.

For the economic rationalists, front-end resourcing provides substantial back-end savings of public money.

FRONT END (AGAIN)

Likewise with other matters that have been examined in this book:

- if we put more into the front end of resolving youth and domestic problems we save more later;
- if we put more into crime prevention we save on dealing with the consequences of crime;
- if we treat drug addicts for their health and social problems they avoid becoming criminals.

As I have stated, criminal punishment, especially imprisonment, despite all the platitudes mouthed regularly and as a matter of course by sentencing courts, successfully deters only a very small handful of offenders. Maybe a couple of per cent, as studies have suggested. Despite that, however, the NSW Government announced in December 1999 and January 2000 that a new men's prison is to be built to house 350 prisoners at Kempsey and a new women's prison to house

200 at Windsor. The spin put on the Kempsey story was that it would provide regional employment in both construction and operation and that it would benefit prisoners and their families who come from the north coast. Wow!

Was there any word about why we need more prisons? About the fact that the existing prisons have been operating at well over 100 per cent capacity for some time? About why it is that the prison population is growing at such a rate? About what we might more effectively do to prevent people becoming prisoners in the first place? No. We continue to fill the bucket.

The prisons bucket cost New South Wales $473.3 million in 1998–99, up more than $40 million on the previous year. A new prison costs about $75 million to build and about $25 million per year to run. Couldn't that sort of money be better spent? Perhaps by paying closer attention to some of the signs that are already there. (But there are none so blind as those who will not see . . .)

DNA

DNA (deoxyribonucleic acid), the building block of life. A great big flashing neon sign for criminal law enforcement!

Each of us has our own unique DNA. It is in our cells. We are not very protective of it and we pass it on, even in a handshake. It is in our blood, saliva, in seminal fluid, in vaginal secretions, in our sweat. Wherever a bodily substance or secretion is left behind at a crime scene the DNA in it can be identified and matched with DNA from any sample of a bodily substance or secretion provided by or obtained from the perpetrator.

An individual's DNA profile can be obtained from a lick

on a cotton swab. It can be identified as having come from him or her alone, to a mathematical probability that makes it, for all practical purposes, certain.

What a wonderful crime-fighting tool! If we truly accept that the criminal justice process should be searching for the truth, what a wonderfully easy way of identifying a particular person from blood, a bit of spit, sweat, some semen, a hair root, a bit of skin, fingernail, urine, faeces — any bodily substance or excretion.

And what a wonderfully easy way of excluding the innocent!

The United Kingdom has established a national DNA database, building a bank of DNA samples from cotton swabs rubbed in the mouths of people who have been arrested. It should be remembered that about 90 per cent of crime in the UK is committed by about 10 per cent of the population. There are now about 650 000 people (1 per cent of the population) on the database and the authorities now get between 400 and 700 matches per week from the examination of crime scenes and victims. Thirty-four unsolved homicides have been resolved already in a few years by matching new people against old crime scene samples. What a clearup score! There has now been a decision in Australia to implement Crimtrac, including a national DNA database, but we are still talking ... in meetings of Police Commissioners, in meetings of Police Ministers, of Attorneys General, in meetings of those who are committed to the expansion of DNA testing but whose hands are tied until their masters (those Commissioners, Police Ministers and Attorneys General) put the decision into action.

There are eight police forces in Australia (the ACT also uses the Australian Federal Police). Each one wants to do things its way. There are nine governments (not counting local government). Each of those wants to follow its own program and procedures, coinciding with others almost by accident. The divisions in our federal system are as much an obstacle to the realisation of a goal like a national DNA database as is the alleged shortage of funding for such a worthwhile purpose.

Within each government system there is a collection of departments and agencies that all want to do things their way, that all have their own individual priorities and financial imperatives and that rarely cooperate in a common goal.

In the meantime, the overstretched NSW Health Department (the priority of which is definitely not testing DNA samples for criminal prosecutions) has three operational DNA scientists working like steam (for a population of about 6.5 million). In South Australia (population 1.5 million) there are five, plus two technicians. In Victoria (population 4.7 million) there are 17. And in the Province of Quebec, Canada (population about the same as NSW) — 58! Ah . . . the clever country!

It has been calculated that for an annual expenditure of between $5 million to $10 million for a facility testing 25 000 samples per annum, New South Wales could (after an initial operating period of about two years in which a database would be built up) solve an additional 120 to 150 crimes per week by DNA matching. Worth the money?

This is 'stuff' that we have now that can also be the stuff of the future. For a very small investment now, Australia is in the position of being able to make enormous gains in the future, solving crimes by extremely cost-effective methods and providing the satisfaction to victims and the community of knowing that offenders are identified and dealt with and the innocent excluded. DNA matching in most cases means pleas of guilty and the subsequent savings of money, time and anguish that the operation of the criminal justice system entails. It can clear up an enormous number of crimes without any increase in police powers. Intelligence-led policing.

Its use will have some general deterrent effect on offenders. There will be a greater probability of detection for many types of crime. That is what deters, when deterrence is a possibility at all, the expectation of being caught.

The use of DNA matching should be introduced after proper community consultation, with appropriate safeguards in place to ensure that the information is not abused or used for any ulterior purpose. There are privacy concerns here, but these were overcome for fingerprints and they have been overcome elsewhere for DNA. Now is the time for action, including involvement of the community in supporting the initiative.

A FINAL WORD

To operate effectively in any society, the criminal law and the criminal justice process must be acceptable to the public and the public must have confidence in it. Not confidence that it will always get it right, or that it will always produce the result that they would like to see, but confidence that it is better than any sensible and realistic alternative that they are able to come up with. In short, the public must be content to hand over to the system the justice that they would otherwise try to achieve on their own.

Without that confidence our criminal justice system would be worse than useless, because it would not be supported and would be bypassed or ignored. Then we would all be at risk.

Those who trivialise a very complex and substantially effective system by constantly seeking to 'toughen' it, ignore its capabilities and achievements and the factors that bring people into it in the first place. We don't need more police powers, they are already adequate. We don't need severer sentences, that would only increase the cost to the community of dealing with more prisoners. We don't need more prisons *if* we adopt more sensible courses of action long before it comes to that.

Instead of talking tough, let's talk smart. Let's put the talk-back 'entertainers' to work uncovering the experts who really do know what they are talking about, exposing their views and encouraging the community — all of us — to discuss more sensibly the alternatives that really are capable of making a difference to the level of our relaxation and comfort. There is enough sensation about without manufacturing more around the criminal justice system.

And let's have the politicians, supported by the electorate who make their informed views known to their representatives, focus on areas where their policies and legislation can actually make a difference (even if that might not occur before the next election).

Before they all say 'do', let them all ask 'why?'

Appendix: Universal Declaration of Human Rights

*Adopted and proclaimed by General
Assembly resolution 217 A (III) of
10 December 1948*

PREAMBLE

Whereas recognition of the inherent dignity and of the equal
and inalienable rights of all members of the human family is
the foundation of freedom, justice and peace in the world,

Whereas disregard and contempt for human rights have
resulted in barbarous acts which have outraged the conscience of mankind, and the advent of a world in which
human beings shall enjoy freedom of speech and belief and
freedom from fear and want has been proclaimed as the
highest aspiration of the common people,

Whereas it is essential, if man is not to be compelled to
have recourse, as a last resort, to rebellion against tyranny
and oppression, that human rights should be protected by
the rule of law,

Whereas it is essential to promote the development of
friendly relations between nations,

Whereas the peoples of the United Nations have in the

Charter reaffirmed their faith in fundamental human rights, in the dignity and worth of the human person and in the equal rights of men and women and have determined to promote social progress and better standards of life in larger freedom,

Whereas Member States have pledged themselves to achieve, in co-operation with the United Nations, the promotion of universal respect for and observance of human rights and fundamental freedoms,

Whereas a common understanding of these rights and freedoms is of the greatest importance for the full realization of this pledge,

Now, therefore,

The General Assembly

Proclaims this Universal Declaration of Human Rights as a common standard of achievement for all peoples and all nations, to the end that every individual and every organ of society, keeping this Declaration constantly in mind, shall strive by teaching and education to promote respect for these rights and freedoms and by progressive measures, national and international, to secure their universal and effective recognition and observance, both among the peoples of Member States themselves and among the peoples of territories under their jurisdiction.

Article 1

All human beings are born free and equal in dignity and rights. They are endowed with reason and conscience and should act towards one another in a spirit of brotherhood.

Article 2

Everyone is entitled to all the rights and freedoms set forth in this Declaration, without distinction of any kind, such as race, colour, sex, language, religion, political or other opinion, national or social origin, property, birth or other status.

Furthermore, no distinction shall be made on the basis of the political, jurisdictional or international status of the country or territory to which a person belongs, whether it be independent, trust, non-self-governing or under any other limitation of sovereignty.

Article 3

Everyone has the right to life, liberty and security of person.

Article 4

No one shall be held in slavery or servitude; slavery and the slave trade shall be prohibited in all their forms.

Article 5

No one shall be subjected to torture or to cruel, inhuman or degrading treatment or punishment.

Article 6

Everyone has the right to recognition everywhere as a person before the law.

Article 7

All are equal before the law and are entitled without any discrimination to equal protection of the law. All are entitled to equal protection against any discrimination in violation of this Declaration and against any incitement to such discrimination.

Article 8

Everyone has the right to an effective remedy by the competent national tribunals for acts violating the fundamental rights granted him by the constitution or by law.

Article 9

No one shall be subjected to arbitrary arrest, detention or exile.

Article 10

Everyone is entitled in full equality to a fair and public hearing by an independent and impartial tribunal, in the determination of his rights and obligations and of any criminal charge against him.

Article 11

1. Everyone charged with a penal offence has the right to be presumed innocent until proved guilty according to law in a public trial at which he has had all the guarantees necessary for his defence.

2. No one shall be held guilty of any penal offence on account of any act or omission which did not constitute a penal offence, under national or international law, at the time when it was committed. Nor shall a heavier penalty be imposed than the one that was applicable at the time the penal offence was committed.

Article 12

No one shall be subjected to arbitrary interference with his privacy, family, home or correspondence, nor to attacks upon his honour and reputation. Everyone has the right to the protection of the law against such interference or attacks.

Article 13

1. Everyone has the right to freedom of movement and residence within the borders of each State.

2. Everyone has the right to leave any country, including his own, and to return to his country.

Article 14

1. Everyone has the right to seek and to enjoy in other countries asylum from persecution.

2. This right may not be invoked in the case of prosecutions genuinely arising from non-political crimes or from acts contrary to the purposes and principles of the United Nations.

Article 15

1. Everyone has the right to a nationality.

2. No one shall be arbitrarily deprived of his nationality nor denied the right to change his nationality.

Article 16

1. Men and women of full age, without any limitation due to race, nationality or religion, have the right to marry and to found a family. They are entitled to equal rights as to marriage, during marriage and at its dissolution.

2. Marriage shall be entered into only with the free and full consent of the intending spouses.

3. The family is the natural and fundamental group unit of society and is entitled to protection by society and the State.

Article 17

1. Everyone has the right to own property alone as well as in association with others.

2. No one shall be arbitrarily deprived of his property.

Article 18

Everyone has the right to freedom of thought, conscience

and religion; this right includes freedom to change his religion or belief, and freedom, either alone or in community with others and in public or private, to manifest his religion or belief in teaching, practice, worship and observance.

Article 19
Everyone has the right to freedom of opinion and expression; this right includes freedom to hold opinions without interference and to seek, receive and impart information and ideas through any media and regardless of frontiers.

Article 20
1. Everyone has the right to freedom of peaceful assembly and association.

2. No one may be compelled to belong to an association.

Article 21
1. Everyone has the right to take part in the government of his country, directly or through freely chosen representatives.

2. Everyone has the right to equal access to public service in his country.

3. The will of the people shall be the basis of the authority of government; this will shall be expressed in periodic and genuine elections which shall be by universal and equal suffrage and shall be held by secret vote or by equivalent free voting procedures.

Article 22
Everyone, as a member of society, has the right to social security and is entitled to realization, through national effort and international co-operation and in accordance with the

organization and resources of each State, of the economic, social and cultural rights indispensable for his dignity and the free development of his personality.

Article 23

1. Everyone has the right to work, to free choice of employment, to just and favourable conditions of work and to protection against unemployment.

2. Everyone, without any discrimination, has the right to equal pay for equal work.

3. Everyone who works has the right to just and favourable remuneration ensuring for himself and his family an existence worthy of human dignity, and supplemented, if necessary, by other means of social protection.

4. Everyone has the right to form and to join trade unions for the protection of his interests.

Article 24

Everyone has the right to rest and leisure, including reasonable limitation of working hours and periodic holidays with pay.

Article 25

1. Everyone has the right to a standard of living adequate for the health and well-being of himself and of his family, including food, clothing, housing and medical care and necessary social services, and the right to security in the event of unemployment, sickness, disability, widowhood, old age or other lack of livelihood in circumstances beyond his control.

2. Motherhood and childhood are entitled to special care and assistance. All children, whether born in or out of wedlock, shall enjoy the same social protection.

Article 26

1. Everyone has the right to education. Education shall be free, at least in the elementary and fundamental stages. Elementary education shall be compulsory. Technical and professional education shall be made generallay available and higher education shall be equally accessible to all on the basis of merit.

2. Education shall be directed to the full development of the human personality and to the strengthening of respect for human rights and fundamental freedoms. It shall promote understanding, tolerance and friendship among all nations, racial or religious groups, and shall further the activities of the United Nations for the maintenance of peace.

3. Parents have a prior right to choose the kind of education that shall be given to their children.

Article 27

1. Everyone has the right freely to participate in the cultural life of the community, to enjoy the arts and to share in scientific advancement and its benefits.

2. Everyone has the right to the protection of the moral and material interests resulting from any scientific, literary or artistic production of which he is the author.

Article 28

Everyone is entitled to a social and international order in which the rights and freedoms set forth in this Declaration can be fully realized.

Article 29

1. Everyone has duties to the community in which alone the free and full development of his personality is possible.

2. In the exercise of his rights and freedoms, everyone shall be subject only to such limitations as are determined by law solely for the purpose of securing due recognition and respect for the rights and freedoms of others and of meeting the just requirements of morality, public order and the general welfare in a democratic society.

3. These rights and freedoms may in no case be exercised contrary to the purposes and principles of the United Nations.

Article 30

Nothing in this Declaration may be interpreted as implying for any State, group or person any right to engage in any activity or to perform any act aimed at the destruction of any of the rights and freedoms set forth herein.

Acknowledgements

Rudyard Kipling wrote, 'There is none like to me, says the cub, in the pride of his earliest kill. But the jungle is large and the cub, he is small; let him think and be still'.

I have inhabited the large jungle of the criminal law for a long time, but I am a cub in the jungle of publishing. This book is a first kill — I am thinking about it — and I am still. As the second-rate comedian said, 'He is a very modest man; and he has a lot to be modest about'.

That this book exists at all is due to Patrick Gallagher, Allen & Unwin's managing director, who wrote me a note challenging me to turn some *Australian Financial Review* musings into a full-scale book. That I actually finished the book is due to John Iremonger, urger, whose dogged wheedling meant that my spare time evaporated. Rebecca Kaiser, editorial manager, took it over near the end and Mary Rennie, editor, made invaluable suggestions (some of which were adopted). For all that, I take full responsibility for the bad bits.

The bulk of this work was completed by mid-2000. I have

relied upon many sources of information: the media itself (but not the talkback voices), journals, reports and submissions. A deliberate choice has been made not to annotate the writing or to give it the features or even the appearance of an academic work. This is a discussion prompter (I hope) that should be read easily.

My thanks to Allen & Unwin.

Index

driving offences
  education campaigns
    against 74
  no obligation to disclose
    defence 93–4
  sentencing guidelines for
    119–20
drug abuse 29–44
  effect on crime rates 78, 84
  help and support for
    victims 40
  prevention of 146
drug sellers
  as career criminals 37
  ethnic backgrounds 31
  financial pressures on 33
  reducing profits of 39
Drug Summit (NSW) 42–4

economic disadvantage *see*
  poverty
economic issues
  cost of drug use 30, 32–3
  cost of prisons 147
  domestic violence 72
  effect on crime rates 79
  in criminal justice 141
  in juvenile justice 64
  making heroin available to
    addicts 38–40
  prison populations 80
ecstasy, seizures of 34
education
  about domestic violence
    74–5
  about drug use 35, 39
  effect on juvenile crime 55

  role in preventing crime 47,
    86
  teaches social control
    82–3
elections, law and order
  campaigns in 21–3, 106
Ending Domestic Violence?
  Programs for
  Perpetrators 74
errors in trials, appeals
  against 17
ethnic backgrounds
  crime rates 78
  domestic violence 72
  drug sellers 31
  mandatory sentencing 109,
    111
European Court of Human
  Rights 57–8
European Union rights
  clauses 134
evidence
  admissions as 91
  called by prosecution 13
  called during committal 12
  child sexual abuse cases
    62
  considered by prosecution
    8–9
  non-disclosure by defence
    91–2, 94
  prosecution obliged to make
    available 91
  role in investigation 6
executive arm of government
  3–4
expert witnesses 93